SUN VALLEY CELEBRITY ★ & LOCAL HEROES COOKBOOK

Compiled by Sheila K. Liermann
Edited by Nancy Reid

as a benefit for

The ADVOCATES  ™

Peak Media, Inc. Publishing

The proceeds from the sale of this book will be returned to
The Advocates for use in aiding victims of domestic violence.

For additional copies, please use the order blank at the back of the book or write directly to:

The Advocates
P.O. Box 3216
Hailey, ID 83333

Telephone (208) 788-4191

Checks should be made payable to The Advocates
for the amount of $12.00 plus $4.00 postage and handling per copy.

The Advocates cookbook may be obtained by retail outlets at special rates.
Write for further information.

Cover and interior art by Will Caldwell

Published by
Peak Media, Inc.
P.O. Box 511, Fairfield, ID 83327
Telephone (208)764-3100
Printed in Korea
Creative Director: Mark Kashino
Art Director: Judy Guryan

Third Printing

SBN 0-9639134-3-3

Thank You, Thank You, Thank You

Thank you for purchasing the Sun Valley Celebrity and Local Heroes Cookbook. I hope you have as much fun reading the book as you do cooking from it and as I did compiling it. The cookbook tries to acknowledge many of the colorful and uncommon people that celebrate life and make the Wood River Valley a special place to live and visit.

Warm hearted thanks to each of the contributors who took time from movie sets, rock tours, athletic training and the demands of a full life to submit a recipe. Without each of you, there wouldn't be anyone else to thank!!

Before we had one recipe, a publisher, or financial backing, a couple of local people generously offered help. Chip Stanek, Jan Burrell and Dave Anderson of Sawtooth Title donated unlimited use of their copy machine. Carol and Malcolm Graham, owners of Wood River Office Supply, contributed over 700 manila envelopes and other supplies. These gestures really got the cookbook off the ground and mean much to a group that has little money set aside for fund raising. Thanks for your belief that the cookbook would one day be part of the inventory of local bookstores.

A special thanks to Susie Beaulaurier Graetz, editor of the Montana Celebrity Cookbook, for sharing her experiences and letting me pick her brain. I may never have started on this endeavor if Susie hadn't been so generous with her secrets.

Special thanks to Andy Phillips, a banker who wears a Wrangler attitude instead of a polyester one and understands the "high-finance" (or lack of it) of non-profit groups.

Recognizing that art can be a vehicle for social change, Will Caldwell has always been generous with his time and talent. Thanks again, Will. Only you could have created the art for this cookbook.

Thanks to Julie Driver and Nancy Reid, Co-Presidents of The Advocates. You two are like the anchor store in a mall, a cold beer at the end of a hard day. Ladies, you really do hold it all together. Thanks from all of The Advocates.

Over time it seemed that our Savant office gradually turned into the "cookbook headquarters." Thanks to Bill McMahan for tolerating the phone calls, deliveries, faxes, interruptions, etc.

Bigger than life thanks to Nancy Reid, in her capacity as chief editor and humorist. Thanks, Nanc, for keeping the project on track by having panic attacks at different times than I had panic attacks and more importantly, thank you for your journalistic skills. And, baby Sofia, thanks for being loyal to your nap time so your mom and I could work. A hug to Shirley and Krishan Anderson for entertaining and watching over Sofia when she was awake!

Thanks to Tom Diggins and the Ketchum Post Office for pushing the confines of bureaucracy to the limit.

The cookbook as it now appears certainly isn't the same mess of faxes, copies, and widespread chaos that I delivered to Mark Kashino and Judy Guryan of Peak Media. Thanks to Mark and Judy for their patience, artistic flair, general good taste and a sometimes irreverent wit, which I most appreciate.

Lastly, thanks to my darlin' Ray, aka Two Dog, who cheerfully tolerated my complete neglect of our kitchen during the months it took to amass these recipes. Life wouldn't be the same without your banter!

Sheila Liermann

Special thanks to the following good folks who hounded or humored recipes from their friends:

Heidi Baldwin, Deb Barrymore, Edie Baskin, Rich Bray, Darlene Byington, Julie Caldwell, Sandra Caulkins, Darlene Crawford, Sherry Daech, Julie Driver, Nicki Foster, Annette Frehling, Wendy Jaquet, Dennis Kavanagh, Deborah Lewis, Cindy Mattson, Penny Mazzola, Ken Oclassen, Linda O'Shea, Patty Provonsha, Nancy Reid, Kate Ryan, Suzy St. Clair, Gene Steiner, Gary Storey, Betty Swanson, Charlotte Thompson, Hillary White and Susan Winget

The printing of this cookbook was made possible by a loan from

WEST ONE
BANK Twin Falls, Idaho
and Andy Phillips, Vice President.

Thanks to the anonymous Ketchum angels for generously guaranteeing the loan.

The Advocates

The Advocates for Survivors of Domestic Violence is a non-profit group committed to the idea that all Wood River families deserve to live in safety and dignity.

The Advocates have helped hundreds of families through their counseling and support group programs, court advocacy and crisis hotline. With a 24-hour crisis hotline, each volunteer advocate is at the front line of domestic violence.

Advocates respond to crises at the hospital, the police station or where ever they are needed to offer women or men the options they need to make healthy decisions in their lives.

Dedication

The Advocates dedicate this book to families whose lives are overshadowed by emotional and physical violence. And to the survivors who have had the courage and tenacity to overcome their circumstances.

Table of Contents

Trail Creek Traffic Jam

Starcraft Enterprises
233 Emerald Bay
Laguna Beach, CA 92651
Tel: 714-494-8181
FAX: 714-497-0999

Buzz Aldrin
Astronaut

LOIS: 714-494-4022
Cellular: 213-718-3821
Los Angeles: 310-274-2181
Sun Valley Tel: 208-622-3883
Sun Valley Fax: 208-622-5520

BUZZ'S LUNAR LANDING HONEY MARINADE

1 steak (Flank, Chateau Briand, etc.) to serve 6
1/2 cup soy sauce   1 tsp. powdered ginger
3 tbsp. honey   1-1/2 tbsp. garlic powder
3/4 cup canola oil   sesame seeds
2 tbsp. vinegar

Pierce steak with fork so that marinade can penetrate. Blend all ingredients together (except sesame seeds) and marinate the meat for at least 10 hours or overnight. Broil or barbecue approximately 7 minutes per side, depending upon thickness of steak. Slice on diagonal and sprinkle with sesame seeds.

CAPE CANAVERAL KEY LIME-BASIL VINAIGRETTE

1 egg   2 - 3 garlic cloves
1/2 cup olive oil   2 tablespoons fresh parsley
1/2 cup canola oil   a fistful of basil leaves
1/3 cup red wine vinegar   salt & freshly ground pepper
1 tablespoon key lime juice

Whiz the egg in a blender until light-colored. Add the garlic, salt, pepper and herbs and continue processing until herbs are finely chopped. Gradually add the oils and key lime juice until well blended. Chill before serving.

Buzz Aldrin

On July 20, 1969, the world stopped as 550 million people watched Buzz Aldrin
and Neil Armstrong become the first two humans to walk on the moon. After Buzz returned,
he was presented with the Presidential Medal of Freedom and authored several books on
space exploration. Buzz and wife Lois enjoy deep-sea scuba diving
and skiing the mountain tops of Sun Valley.

❄❄ ZUCCHINI BREAD ❄❄

This zucchini bread recipe is special because I make it during the holidays to give as a Christmas gift to my family and friends. This is one of my father's favorite gifts at Christmas time.

Ingredients:

3 eggs
1 cup oil
2 cups sugar
2 cups grated zucchini
2 tsp. baking soda
1/2 tbsp. baking powder
3 cups flour

1/4 tsp. cloves
3 tsp. cinnamon
1/4 tsp. nutmeg
2 tsp. vanilla
1 tsp. salt
1 cup walnuts
1 cup raisins

Mix dry ingredients together in a medium size bowl. In a separate large bowl, beat the eggs until foamy. Add oil, sugar, and vanilla to the eggs. Now, stir dry ingredients into the egg mixture. Next, add grated zucchini (including excess juice) to mixture. Last, but not least, add the walnuts and raisins and you're ready to pop it in the oven.

Bake at 325 degrees for one hour. Makes 2 bread loaves.

I hope you enjoy this bread as much as I do. Happy eating!

Adele Allender

Adele Allender, another Sun Valley Ski Education Foundation prodigy, was a member of the U.S. Alpine Ski Team for six years, and the World Championship Alpine Team for two years. In 1990, Adele was the National Collegiate Skiing Association champion. Adele says Baldy is "the best mountain in the world."

HOME ALONE WHITE BEANS
By helcia

I always have a supply of staples on hand for those days when friends stop by, or I'm home alone and want to feel a little special. My pantry is always stocked with the following:

White beans, cannellini, or great northern ... also canned whites for fast preparation. Extra virgin olive oil, garlic cloves, bay leaf, thyme, sage, rosemary, crushed red pepper, tomatoes, red onion, Parmesan cheese, and always a good French bottle of wine (just in case the recipe doesn't come out right)!

Serving for four. I eat two helpings, and it's great warmed up!

1/2 pound dried white beans, rinsed, or 2 cans
3 tbsp. olive oil
3 garlic cloves, chopped
red onion
3 tbsp. parsley, fresh chopped flat leaf is best
smidgen of dried oregano
4 plum tomatoes, peeled & chopped
1 bay leaf
1/2 tsp. crushed red pepper
1 tbsp., fresh, if you have it, thyme, sage & rosemary
1/3 cup fresh basil leaves, torn
freshly grated Parmesan cheese, for serving

OOOO's XXX's
helcia

Soak beans for a few minutes. Bring to boil, then set aside, covered for 1 hour ... or open 2 cans of beans.

Rinse beans and cover them with 1 inch cold water. Bring to a boil, then reduce heat and cook until tender, about 40 minutes.

In sauce pan, add oil, garlic, parsley, thyme, bay leaf, crushed red pepper and oregano. Cook on low heat 3 1/2 minutes. Add 1 cup of cold water (or 1/2 water and 1/2 white wine). Season with salt and freshly ground pepper. Bring to a boil, then cover and simmer 5 minutes.

Stir in tomatoes, gently add beans, then cover and cook for 5 minutes. Remove bay leaf.

Ladle beans and juices into a soup bowl (flat). Place red onion rings on top, sprinkle Parmesan cheese on top. SERVE HOT.

Pour yourself a nice glass of french wine... ahhhhh!

A Matter of Taste

Ketchum's first bistro, A Matter of Taste, is modeled after Norman barns built in the Middle Ages when farmers plastered straw into the walls for warmth. Owner Helcia's entrees reflect old Europe and are inspired by her German family members, a creative kitchen staff and her travels. The bistro's famous French Onion Soup is so packed with cheeses, it is graciously served with a pair of scissors.

PASTA PUTTANESCA

RESTAURANT

"Dedicated To Great Mediterranean Cuisine"

This is the perfect dish to make when you find yourself with a bumper crop of ripe tomatoes. The recipe is said to have originated in Naples, where the ladies of the night would cook huge pots of this spicy, aromatic sauce to lure the sailors up to their quarters. I never tire of Pasta Puttanesca.

6 Servings

2 1/2 pounds ripe tomatoes
4 tbsp. olive oil
4 cloves fresh garlic, minced
1 can anchovy fillets, drained, patted dry and chopped
1/2 cup sliced green olives or pitted Greek olives
2-3 tbsp. capers, chopped with juice
1/4 tsp. red pepper flakes
salt and fresh ground pepper to taste (optional)
1 1/2 pounds spaghettini or fettuccine, cooked al dente
freshly grated Parmesan or chopped parsley (optional)

Blanch, peel, and coarsely chop tomatoes. A food processor can be used. If you're in a hurry, don't bother peeling the tomatoes.

Heat oil in a heavy duty saucepan. Cook garlic until golden. Stir in tomatoes, anchovies, olives, and capers. Season with salt and pepper and cook for 5 minutes over medium high heat.

In a large bowl, toss sauce with pasta and sprinkle with parmesan or parsley.

Bon Appetito!

921 West Jefferson Street • Boise, Idaho 83702 • 208-343-6435

Amore Restaurant

Amore Restaurant is an Italian gastronomic oasis in a sea of fast food restaurants. When Ketchum residents make one of their frequent pilgrimages to Boise's Costco, the regional mall and other retail magnets, a stop at Amore provides the nourishment and encouragement needed to drive home. Owner Rory Farrow lived in the Wood River Valley during the 70s and says, "It has been a part of my life ever since."

Wähe (Swiss Fruit Tart)

This fruit pie is a very popular dish in Switzerland. It is traditionally served for lunch on Friday. This tradition goes back over 300 years to the days when religion forbade eating meat on Fridays, in memory of the death of Christ. Still today, almost every bakery and many of the restaurants offer a wide variety of these pies for lunch.

Piecrust:
- 1 1/2 cups flour
- 2/3 stick butter or margarine, melted
- 6 tbsp. sour cream or yogurt
- 2-3 tbsp. sugar
- 1/2 tsp. salt
- 1-2 tbsp. water, as needed

Filling:
- 2 lbs. (approx) fruit. Use apples, peeled and cut in 1/4's, or halved apricots, plums, or peaches. Chopped rhubarb or cherries is good, too.
- 1/4 to 1/2 cup sugar

Custard:
- 2-3 eggs, beaten lightly
- 1 to 1 1/4 cups milk or half & half
- 1/4 cup sugar
- 1 tbsp. cornstarch
- 1 dash cinnamon

In a bowl or Cusinart, mix the flour with the melted butter, sour cream, sugar, salt and water. Process quickly until the dough forms a ball, or mix with a wooden spoon until dough is smooth. Do not knead. Let rest for 20 minutes in the refrigerator. Another option is to use puff pastry from the grocery store, found mostly in the freezer section.

Roll dough out and press into a greased pie pan (11"-12"). Then double the edge and crimp it. Sprinkle the bottom with some finely ground nuts (optional).

Spread the fruit over the dough and sprinkle it with the sugar. If using tart fruit, like rhubarb or apricots, you might need to increase sugar a little or sprinkle more sugar over the pie halfway through baking time. Pour custard over this and bake at 350° until custard is set, 45 minutes to an hour.

Gabriele Andersen

Gabriele Andersen

Gabriele Andersen's running accomplishments are too numerous to mention here. Highlights include running the marathon in the 1984 Los Angeles Olympics and taking first place in the Heart of San Diego, California International and Twin Cities marathons. She holds many Swiss and U.S. Masters records. Gabriele, born in Switzerland, confesses she breaks training with an "indulgence in Swiss chocolate once in awhile."

OFFICE OF THE GOVERNOR
STATE CAPITOL
BOISE 83720-1000

CECIL D. ANDRUS
GOVERNOR

(208) 334-2100

Carol and I heartily applaud the work of The Advocates for Survivors of Domestic Violence. We wish you every success in your efforts to help the victims and solve the problem of domestic violence in the Wood River Valley.

Cece & Carol Andrus

Pheasant Pie

1 pheasant, 3 to 4 lbs. dressed weight	1 bay leaf
6 peppercorns	1 stalk celery
1 tablespoon salt	1/2 cup butter
1 cup light cream	1/2 cup flour
1/8 teaspoon pepper	1/4 teaspoon salt
1-1 pound can pearl onions (optional)	1 package frozen peas
1-14 ounce can sliced mushrooms	2 canned pimentos, sliced
1 box pastry mix	

Place pheasant in large kettle and cover with water. Add bay leaf, celery, peppercorn, and 1 tablespoon salt. Bring to a boil. Cover and cook over low heat 2 to 3 hours, or until pheasant is tender. (Can be done the day before.)

Remove meat from bones; strain broth. Melt butter in saucepan; add flour and stir until blended. Gradually add 2 cups of the broth, stirring constantly. Add light cream, pepper, and salt. Cook, stirring until thickened. Arrange pheasant pieces, onions, mushrooms, peas, and pimentos in 2 quart casserole. Add sauce, leaving at least 1 inch space at top. Prepare pastry mix. Cut pastry circle 1/2 inch larger than casserole and place over pheasant mixture, turning edge of pastry under and pressing to casserole with fork or spoon. Bake in preheated 450 degree oven <u>until crust is golden brown</u> - 15 to 30 minutes or longer if necessary.

Makes 4 to 6 servings.

Cecil Andrus

Cecil Andrus can claim two unprecedented firsts in Idaho history. Governor Andrus is the first person to be elected Idaho governor four times, and as President Carter's Secretary of the Interior, he is the first Idahoan to hold a presidential cabinet post. We hope to see more of "Cece" on the Sun Valley golf course after his retirement.

OFFICE OF THE GOVERNOR

STATE CAPITOL

BOISE 83720-1000

CECIL D. ANDRUS
GOVERNOR

(208) 334-2100

The following cake is a favorite of the Andrus family and has become a tradition at their birthday celebrations.

Three Layer Prune Cake

6 tablespoons butter	3 cups flour	1 1/2 teaspoons salt
2 1/4 cups sugar	3 teaspoons soda	1 1/2 cups sour milk
3/8 cup of prune juice	1 1/2 teaspoons nutmeg	1 1/2 cups cooked prunes
4 eggs	1 1/2 teaspoons cinnamon	(Use Idaho prunes & "Buy Idaho" whenever possible)

Cream butter and sugar. Add prune juice and beaten egg yolks. Sift dry ingredients. Stir into first mixture, alternately with sour milk. Fold in beaten egg whites and cut up prunes. Bake in 3 layers for 30 to 40 minutes at 350 degrees. Cool and frost with chocolate frosting.
(For sour milk, use 1 tbsp. vinegar to 1 cup milk.)

Frosting for Prune Cake

1/2 cup butter	1/2 cup nutmeats (if desired)
4 cups powdered sugar (sifted)	2 egg yolks
2 or 3 squares melted chocolate	2 teaspoons vanilla
6 tablespoons cream	

Cream butter and 1/2 cup powdered sugar. Add melted chocolate, egg yolks, and vanilla. Stir in remaining sugar, adding cream as frosting becomes thick.

Cece & Carol Andrus

Carol Andrus

As Idaho's First Lady, Carol Andrus has distinguished herself by consistent advocacy of policies and programs that improve the quality of life for Idaho's children. Among her many community and civic commitments are membership in the March of Dimes, Mothers Against Drunk Driving, Family Advocate Program Board of Directors and an Advisory Board of the Department of Health and Welfare.

ANIMAL SHELTER
OF WOOD RIVER VALLEY
A NON-PROFIT CORPORATION

<u>CHILI RELLENOS</u>

3-4 cans chile peppers
1 lb. Tillamook or Cheddar Cheese
1 lb. Monterey Jack Cheese
4 eggs
13 oz. can of condensed milk
3 tsp. flour
1 tsp. salt
2 - 8 oz. cans tomato sauce

Wash and remove seeds and drain peppers.
Grate cheese and put in piles. Place chilies
flat in pan, cover with yellow cheese, then
chilies and then jack cheese. Repeat.
Separate eggs. Beat yolks and add milk,
flour and salt. Beat egg whites and fold in.
Pour over cheese and chilies.

Bake 1 hour at 325. Pour tomato sauce over
and bake 10 more minutes.

E. Gile Williams
President
Animal Shelter of Wood River Valley

Box 1496 • Hailey, Idaho 83333 • 208/788-4351

Animal Shelter

The Animal Shelter of Wood River Valley strives to find families for every animal they receive,
sometimes keeping animals for weeks or months at a time. Fund raising for the shelter began in 1972,
and it opened in May 1982. The shelter is funded by the community, and doesn't take a red cent
from any government agency. Over the years, the shelter has even found homes for sheep
and turned foxes over to wildlife rehabilitators.

JAN ARONSON

I was born and raised in New Orleans and the Creole tradition is the base of much of my cooking. My recipes are healthy and rich in flavor. This casserole can be prepared 3 ways: as a vegetarian dish, or as a seafood or chicken main course.

CREOLE CASSEROLE (serves 6)

Vegetable oil
3 stalks celery, finely chopped
2 large onions, finely chopped
1 large green pepper, finely chopped
1 large red pepper, finely chopped
8 cloves garlic, finely chopped
1/2 pound mushrooms, finely chopped

2 medium sized eggplants, diced with skin and steamed till medium soft.
1 bunch parsley, finely chopped

1/8 teaspoon cayenne pepper
3 tablespoons dried basil
1 tablespoon dried thyme
2 tablespoons dried oregano
1 teaspoon cloves
salt and pepper to taste

breadcrumbs

For Seafood
2 lbs scallops
2 lbs shrimp
2 steamed lobsters (optional) or
1 1/2 lbs monkfish or other firm fish

For Chicken
6 whole chicken breasts cut into 1 inch cubes.

Heat large heavy skillet. When hot reduce heat to medium. Spray with Pam and add a small amount of oil. Add celery, onions, green and red pepper and saute' for about 4 minutes or until vegetables are nearly soft. Add garlic and mushrooms and saute' for another 5 minutes. Add the steamed eggplant and the parsley and stir well. Add the cayenne, basil, thyme, oregano, cloves and salt and pepper to taste. Cook and stir until flavors are blended and vegetable mixture is spoonable but not dry.

If using as a vegetarian dish, Spray a large serving casserole with Pam and add eggplant mixture. Sprinkle top with breadcrumbs and heat in a 350 degree oven for 20-30 minutes or
till hot.

If using seafood, wash scallops well to rid them of sand, Shell, devain, and rinse shrimp. If using lobster, cut meat into chunks. Cut other fish into chunks. In another large skillet saute' separately, in a small amount of oil, the scallops, shrimp and the white fish until just done. Add the lobster and stir. Add the seafood to the eggplant mixture and combine well. Spoon into large casserole which has been sprayed with Pam and sprinkle with breadcrumbs. Bake at 350 for 25-30 minutes or until hot.

For chicken casserole, saute' chicken in a small amount of oil untill cooked through. Add to eggplant mixture and mix well. Spoon into a large casserole which has been sprayed with Pam, sprinkle with breadcrumbs and bake for 25-30 minutes.

960 Fifth Avenue • New York, New York 10021
Home: 212-517-3308 • Studio: 718-472-0412

Jan Aronson

Artist Jan Aronson says, "My work allows me to discover the way I see." And her work takes her all over the globe from trekking in the Sinai to the Himalyas and Patagonia. Yet, Jan draws on what she sees in Idaho and the Wood River Valley as subjects for many of her paintings. Jan's art is owned by collectors from coast to coast, and she has gallery affiliations with the Graham Modern Gallery in New York and the Anne Reed Gallery in Ketchum.

East Fork Associates

NANCY'S SOUR CREAM APPLE PIE

CRUST
1 3/4 Cups Flour
1/4 Cup Sugar
1 Teaspoon Cinnamon
1/2 Teaspoon Salt
2/3 Cup Butter
Apple Cider (or water),
   enough to bind dough

TOPPING
1/2 Cup (1 stick) Butter room temperature
1/2 Cup Flour
1/3 Cup White Sugar
1/3 Cup Brown Sugar
1 Tablespoon Cinnamon
1/4 Teaspoon Salt
1 Cupt Chopped Walnuts

FILLING
1 1/2 Cups Sour Cream
1 Large Egg
1 Cup Sugar
1/4 Cup Flour
2 Teaspoons Vanilla Extract
1/2 Teaspoons Salt
2 1/2 Pounds McIntosh Apples
   pared, cored and sliced (allow
   6 large or 9 small apples)

OVEN
Preheat 450 degrees (reduce to 350
   after 10 minutes of baking)

PIE PAN
One 10 inch

TO PREPARE CRUST
Combine flour sugar, cinnamon and salt.
Cut in butter with pastry blender or fingertips to consistency of course meal.
Add just enough apple cider, one tablespoon at a time to moisten pastry. Use as little
as possible.
Press dough into ball. Roll out and turn into 10-inch Pie Pan.

TO PREPARE FILLING
Combine sour cream, egg, sugar, flour, vanilla and salt in bowl.
Add sliced apples into mixture, stirring to coat.
Turn filling mixture into pie shell just before placing into preheated 450-degree oven.
Bake 10 minutes, then reduce to 350 degrees for 35-40 minutes.

TO PREPARE TOPPING
Blend together butter, flour, white sugar, brown sugar, cinnamon, salt and walnuts.

After pie is baked, remove and stir filling in crust gently but thoroughly. Place topping
evenly over top of pie. Return to oven (at 350 degrees) and bake for 15 minutes more.
Allow finished pie to cool before slicing. Makes one 10-inch pie.

Wayne Badovinus

Wayne Badovinus • P.O. Box 5834 Ketchum, Idaho 83340 • (208) 788-5749 Fax (208) 788-5749

Wayne Badovinus
Next time you slip on those jeans that fit perfectly and that beat-up coat you could never
take to the Gold Mine, thank Wayne Badovinus, former Eddie Bauer Chief Executive Officer.
Previously, Wayne headed up the equally successful Williams-Sonoma.
Wayne, now retired, and wife Nancy collect cowboy and Indian art.

This recipe tastes best when the fish has been out of the water for less than 12 hours, and there is a full moon rising over the Sea of Cortes.

DORADO RICARDO

2 lbs. of filleted Dorado (Mahi Mahi, dolphin fish)
1/4 cup olive oil
1/4 cup vinegar
4 oz. can of Herdez Salsa Mexicana (mild)
1 lime
1 tsp. garlic powder
2 cups mayonnaise (high octane, no light stuff)
1 tbsp. dill

Do NOT run water over fish fillets. Remove moisture by patting dry with paper towel. Locate and remove any bones by carefully running fingers over fish.

Make a double layer foil boat about 1/2 inch deep. Mix ingredients in a blender or beat well with fork. Coat foil with layer of mixture before putting fish in boat. Cover generously with sauce. Do not cover.

Slide the foil boat onto a flat pan, bread board, etc. (usually takes two people for this move). Slide the foil boat onto an already hot barbecue and close the lid. Cook for 10 to 20 minutes depending on the thickness of the fillets. After 10 minutes, check the fish with a sharp point of a knife. Remove when soft. Do not overcook. Fish is done when the center is white.

Remember to use two people to quickly slide the foil boat from the hot grill to the flat board or pan. Careful to not burn knuckles. Serve immediately with a bottle of cold Pacifico or Corona.

Dick Barrymore

Dick Barrymore

Dick Barrymore has produced more than 100 ski movies, beginning in 1960 with *Ski West Young Man* to the 1985 hit *Heli-High*. Since retiring from the sports film industry, Dick has developed a beach resort in Cabo Pulmo, Baja California, Mexico. At the tail end of a long cold winter, Ketchumites are lured like lemmings to this "Sun Valley South."

EDIE BASKIN STUDIO

The great thing about these recipes is that I can whip them together after working a 10-hour day ... then I have time to sit by the river and relax and eat. Keep all the ingredients on hand — it's great when 6 people suddenly show up for dinner!

Maggie's Caesar Dressing

1 can of anchovies with capers
  (oil included)
1 heaping tsp. dijon mustard
8 squirts Worchester sauce
1 egg (optional)
3 cloves garlic
3 tbs. vinegar
3 tbs. olive oil

Mix all ingredients in blender. Toss onto Romaine lettuce. Sprinkle with croutons and parmesan cheese.

Whore's Pasta

olive oil
2 large cans whole tomatoes
1 10 oz. jar calamata olives (pitted by hand)
1 jar capers
6 squirts anchovy paste or 6 anchovies
garlic to taste
1 package rigatoni or angel hair pasta

Cover bottom of deep frying pan generously with olive oil. Add sliced or minced garlic. Let cook for a minute or two while stirring. Add tomatoes, olives, capers, and anchovies. Cook on medium heat at least 20 minutes. Pour over cooked pasta.

Rosemary Bread

Slice a baguette lengthwise. Brush with olive oil - sprinkle with rosemary. Bake in the oven at 350 until golden brown. Serve sliced in a bread basket.

Edie Baskin

Warm Springs Ranch 764 Upper Warm Springs Road Ketchum, Idaho 83340
Phone 208-726-5041 Fax 208-726-4050

Edie Baskin

Edie Baskin is a three-time Emmy nominee. She is the photographer and a production designer for *Saturday Night Live*. Over the years, Edie has been responsible for much of the show's stage and graphic look. Edie has found refuge at her ranch here for 13 years.

RICHARD BASKIN

BACHELOR'S OATMEAL

1) PLACE SOME OATMEAL IN A CEREAL BOWL
(WHOLE OATMEAL, PREFERABLY; NOT INSTANT)

2) ADD WATER, COVERING OATMEAL
TOSS IN SOME RAISINS, DRIED FRUIT, OR NUTS

3) NUKE FOR 3 MINUTES

4) REMOVE FROM MICROWAVE
ENJOY YOUR FAT-FREE BREAKFAST

913 OCEAN FRONT WALK   VENICE, CALIFORNIA 90291
TELEPHONE (310) 399-3553   FACSIMILE (310) 399-4132

Richard Baskin

Richard Baskin began his career in motion pictures and television at the age of 24 as the composer and producer of the Academy Award-winning score of Robert Altman's *Nashville,* for which he also received a Grammy nomination. He has also directed numerous videos and commercials including the award winning *Charlie Chaplin* IBM spots, and music videos for such artists as Rod Stewart and The Temptations. A longtime environmental and political activist, Richard sits on the board of the Natural Resources Defense Council. He lives in Sun Valley and Los Angeles.

St. Charles Parish

P.O. Box 789   †   Hailey, Idaho 83333   †   (208) 788-3024

GARBANZO & CHORIZO
From the kitchen of Pilar Arriaga Harris, St. Charles parishioner

1 small onion, diced
1 clove garlic, diced
2 Basque chorizos, sliced
2 small potatoes, peeled and sliced
1 tbsp. olive oil
2 cans garbanzo beans

Lightly sauté the onion, garlic, chorizos, and potatoes in the olive oil. Be sure all ingredients are covered with oil.

Add 2 cans garbanzo beans, liquid and all. Add salt to taste.

Simmer till potatoes are cooked. For color, add a little parsley or pimento.

A can of tomato sauce can be added for variety.

This recipe will serve 8.

The Basque in Idaho

Escaping Spanish tyranny and poverty in the 1830s, the Basque people fled the Pyrenees for the western United States. Eventually settling in Idaho, first as gold miners and then as sheep herders, the Basque brought with them a unique language, cuisine and dance tradition. From sheep rancher to Secretary of State, the Basque culture continues to influence Idaho. This recipe is typical of Basque cuisine.

Quinoa Waffles

When I learned a few years ago that most people are both addicted and allergic to wheat, my search for alternatives led me to discover (or rediscover) such grains as amaranth, teff, quinoa, millet, kamut, spelt and buckwheat. I never repeat the same waffle recipe, but the following was a particular success.

2 cups freshly ground organic quinoa flour
1 cup freshly ground organic buckwheat flour
6 tbsp. organic sesame tahini
3 tbsp. lecithin
3 tbsp. ground organic flax seed
2 tbsp. canola oil (expeller pressed)
1 tsp. sea salt

Cook the flax for 20 minutes in 1/2 cup of water. Then stir all ingredients together, adding enough water to make the batter pourable. Cook in a preheated waffle iron until it stops steaming. Enjoy!

Gary Beacom
P.O. Box 2401
Sun Valley, Idaho 83353

Gary Beacom

Gary Beacom continues to amaze crowds at the Sun Valley Ice Shows much as he did when he was the World Pro Figure Skating Champion in 1988. Gary's skating signature is jazzy and robust, and his style is uniquely art deco.

SPANISH OMELET PICNIC LOAF

1 large round loaf of sourdough/French bread
  (a flatter loaf works better - 2 inch loaf)

Split bread horizontally. Partially hollow it out, leaving crust.

Brush inside of crust with olive oil.

Omelet filling:
>   9 scrambled eggs
>   mild sausage or ham
>   garlic
>   sliced onions
>   3/4 tsp. salt
>   1/4 tsp. pepper

Sauté ingredients together and combine into an omelet.

Put omelet into the middle of the bread crust. Wrap in foil.
Heat at 350° for 15 minutes.

Hint hint! To keep loaf warm longer, wrap in newspaper after it has been heated. Great insulation.

Put into your favorite pack with a bottle of champagne, wine or mineral water. Stop at your favorite rest stop along the trails and enjoy!

Mary A. Crofts

Promoting a healthy, active way of life in Blaine County!

POST OFFICE BOX 297 · HAILEY, IDAHO 83333 · TEL 208-788-2117 · FAX 208-788-2168

Blaine County Recreation District

Consisting of 30 continuous miles of paved bikeway, the Wood River and Sun Valley Trail System is one of the longest, most comprehensive separated bike and pedestrian systems in the United States. In 1990, the trail received the Alexander Calder Conservation Award for outstanding partnership in business and conservation and, in 1993, the Outstanding Achievement in Tourism Award from Idaho Governor Cecil Andrus.

KETCHUM ALARM COMPANY

This dish is one of our favorites for hot summer days. It will impress guests with its unique flavors and, most importantly, it's easy to make!

COUSCOUS AND CHICK PEA SALAD

*This salad is fun to eat in the traditional manner:
Just roll up a scoop of salad in a lettuce leaf.*

Makes 4 servings

Salad:
1 3/4 cup water
1/2 tsp. salt
1 cup couscous
1 15-oz. can chick peas (garbanzo beans), drained
2 small red peppers, diced
4 (or so) green onions, sliced
1/2 cup chopped or grated carrots
1/2 cup real salty Greek olives

Mint Vinaigrette:
3/4 cup fresh mint sprig tops (1 1/2 bunches or so)
3 tbsp. white wine vinegar (or whatever you have)
2 good garlic cloves
1 tsp. Dijon mustard
1/4 tsp. sugar
2/3 cup olive oil
6 oz. feta cheese, coarsely crumbled
lettuce leaves (Romano is good)

For salad: Bring water and salt to a boil in a medium saucepan. Add couscous. Remove saucepan from heat; cover and let stand 5 minutes. Transfer couscous to large bowl. Fluff with fork. Add chick peas, red peppers, green onion, carrots and olives to bowl.

For vinaigrette: Finely chop mint with vinegar, garlic, mustard and sugar in food processor. With machine running, slowly pour in olive oil. Process until well blended.

Pour dressing over salad. Toss to distribute vegetables and dressing evenly. Gently mix in feta cheese. Season with salt and pepper.

This salad looks great in a bowl with the salad surrounded by lettuce leaves and a few mint springs on top. The flavor also develops a little more after sitting a few hours, so don't be afraid to make this in advance.

Tom Bowman

Post Office Box 3833 Ketchum, Idaho 83340 Telephone (208) 726-8172

♲ *printed on recycled paper*

Tom Bowman

Tom Bowman was chosen from hundreds of athletes across the country for the
U.S. Rowing Team and competed in the 1981 World Championships in Munich, Germany.
Tom says he eats and drinks anything from "red meat to tofu, and red wine to red zinger."

Company

BURN'S PASTA SALAD

Ingredients:

1 package penne pasta
1 cup chopped yellow onions
2 cups chopped celery
1 cup sliced radish
2 cups shredded cheddar cheese
1/4 cup lite Italian dressing

- Boil pasta - 12 minutes, rinse, let cool.

- Combine pasta with vegies -
  Layer in glass bowl; pasta then vegies - repeat.

- Add dressing and cheese.

- Toss

- Chill for 2 hours.

- Makes 7 - 1 cup servings.

P.O. Box 2338 • Sun Valley, Idaho 83353 U.S.A. • 208-622-3200 • FX 208-622-4488

Bobbie Burns

Hard-core skiers remember The Ski, designed and manufactured in the early 70s by Bobbie Burns.
Watch for an updated version of The Ski to be reintroduced the winter of 1993-1994. In keeping with
Burns' tradition, they will be custom, handmade, wet-wrapped, high-performance boards made in
Ketchum. Bobbie also designs his own clothing label that "fits our environment - elegant yet casual
playwear." Victoria's Secret, Nordstrom, and Bloomingdales are among a few of the
large retailers that contract with Bobbie to design their private labels.

BILL BUTTERFIELD
DIRECTOR OF GOLF
P.G.A. MEMBER

SUN VALLEY COMPANY

SUN VALLEY GOLF RESORT
SUN VALLEY, IDAHO 83353
PHONE 208-622-4111, EXT. 2251

Baked Beans ala Butterfield

3 medium sized cans B&M baked beans
1 16 oz. can pineapple tidbits
1 cup brown sugar
1 can tomato paste
1/2 cup ketchup
4 scallions, chopped
1 green pepper, chopped
12 slices thick bacon, diced & cooked
1 lb. hot dogs, cut into pieces

Combine all ingredients except hot dogs. Bake in a large, covered casserole at 200 for 6 hours. Add hot dogs and cook 2 more hours.

Bill Butterfield

Bill Butterfield

Some people have it made. As golf pro and director at the Sun Valley Golf Course,
and assistant director of the Sun Valley Ski School, Bill Butterfield has spent the last 35 years "working"
on the greens or the slopes. As if that's not tough enough, Bill had to help start up the first ski school at
Coronet Peak in Queenstown, New Zealand. Bill is semi-retired now and teaching golf.

Will Caldwell

**Box 1450
Sun Valley, Idaho 83353
(208)726-9059**

This recipe is a favorite from my dear wife, Julie. I told Julie on the summer night we met in 1977, that I was leaving for a year long African painting safari. I mentioned that maybe she'd like to come along...she did just that.

Loon Wild Rice Salad

8 cups cooked rice (2-1/2 cups uncooked). Use 1/2 wild rice and
1/2 brown or white rice.
2 to 3 medium tomatoes, cored and chopped
2 cups diced artichoke hearts
1 medium red onion, chopped
1 cup sliced black olives
1 7 oz. jar Italian roasted peppers
10 pimento-stuffed olives, sliced
1/2 cup chopped fresh Italian parsley
2/3 cup olive oil
1/3 cup white wine vinegar (or use half lemon juice & half vinegar)
1/2 tsp. onion powder
2 to 3 garlic cloves, minced
1 tsp. dried oregano, crumbled
1 tsp. dried basil, crumbled
Salt and freshly ground pepper

• Cook rice according to directions. Let cool.
• Combine first 8 ingredients in a large bowl.
• Whisk oil, vinegar and spices in small bowl.
• Pour over rice mixture and toss well.
• Cover and refrigerate overnight. Serve chilled.
• Makes 12 servings.
• Variation: Add chopped red, green, or yellow peppers.

Loon Wild Rice *is organically grown and has not been treated with any chemicals, herbicides, pesticides or fertilizers. Loon Wild Rice is naturally produced in the lakes and rivers of Northern Minnesota and distributed in Hailey by the* Loon Wild Rice Company. *Call 788-3363 or check your local market.*

Will Caldwell

Will Caldwell

Will Caldwell says he has spent the past 22 years "living at the world's most desirable address" and the past 17 years as a fine arts painter. Will's incredible oils and pastels beautify our cookbook. His art has taken him all over the world, and and his paintings are owned by Coca Cola Inc., Commercial Bank of Africa, National Bank of Kenya, Susan Saint James and George Lucas. Will's non-painting time is spent with his three children. Will and wife Julie give generously to the community: He is the volunteer chapter president of the Idaho Conservation League, and Julie serves on The Advocates' board, among numerous other commitments.

LYNN CAMPION
Deer Creek Farm

When I was growing up, my family spent many weekends at our ranch in the mountains near Denver. There, my mother showed me how to cook on a wood cookstove. Though I took more interest in tasting than in preparing, I did learn how to cook certain types of beef. Still a favorite to this day, is my mother's pot roast and noodles.

MOM'S POT ROAST AND NOODLES FOR 6 PEOPLE

5-1/2 lbs. shoulder cut beef roast, bone-in (bone is important for flavor)
4 strips of bacon, cooked, with grease left in frying pan
2 carrots, sliced
2 tomatoes, chopped
2 celery stalks, sliced
3 cloves of garlic, chopped
1 onion, sliced and saved for top of roast
1 can consomme and 2 cans of water, or enough to come to top of roast
3/4 lb. wide egg noodles

Prepare this dinner in the morning, and the rest of the day is yours!

Preheat oven to 350.
Flour and season the roast, score it with a fork, and brown each side in the hot bacon grease. Place in a heavy metal roasting pan (iron works best), and surround the meat with vegetables and liquid. Top with sliced onion. Cover and cook for 1 hour at 350, then turn the heat to 225. Later in the day, take half of the juice away and use it for cooking other things.
Add the egg noodles 30 minutes before serving, and let them cook in the juices.
Serve in the pan and let everyone take what they wish.

Lynn Campion

Box 538
Ketchum, Idaho

Lynn Campion

Since moving to the Wood River Valley in 1972, Lynn Campion has donned many hats: wife, mother, professional photographer, ski instructor, volunteer firewoman and surgical technician. Lynn also became nationally recognized in the cutting horse world when she won seven major competitions in the West and Northwest. She is the author of *Training and Showing the Cutting Horse* and is presently working on a novel.

Post Office Box 1557
Sun Valley, Idaho 83353
(208) 622-4226

Post Office Box 55
Los Altos, CA 94023
(415) 948-8033
Message: (415) 694-1118
Mobile: (415) 699-4369

JOE'S HEALTH NUT CARROT CAKE

1/2 cup butter	3/4 cup honey
4 eggs	1 tsp. vanilla
3 cups shredded carrots	1 - 20 oz. can crushed
2 1/2 cups whole wheat pastry flour	pineapple, drained
1 tsp. cinnamon	1 tsp. soda
1 cup chopped walnuts	3/4 tsp. sea salt
(health nuts optional)	1 cup raisins

Mix the butter and the honey until creamy (that's <u>the</u> honey, not <u>your</u> honey). Then blend in the eggs, vanilla, carrot, and pineapple.

Then you mix the dry ingredients together and blend them into the creamy mixture.

Mix in the nuts and raisins (it actually tastes good this way and you really don't have to cook it.) It looks better on the table, though, if you pour the mixture into a greased 9x13 pan and bake at 350° for 35-45 minutes. Let it cool down and frost it with your favorite frosting (cream cheese frosting is great).

Joe Cannon

Joe Cannon has been making Sun Valley audiences laugh and join him in sing-alongs since 1974. He divides his time between his homes in California and Sun Valley. A fitness addict, Joe says, "When I can run 12 miles uphill, I'm in heaven."

pasta with uncooked tomato sauce

This recipe requires wonderful, real tomatoes. Being from the East, I have a difficult time out here finding anything resembling the juice-dribbling-down-your-chin tomatoes I used to pick from my garden, but there are farm stands here in the summer, and it's worth the time to drive a little way to buy them.

ingredients

7 large, ripe tomatoes	3 cloves of garlic
1/3 cup fresh basil	1/4 cup fresh Italian parsley
1/3 cup olive oil	1/2 cup grated fontina cheese
salt & pepper to taste	1 lb. pasta

1) Put 5 tomatoes, garlic, basil, parsley, and olive oil in food processor. Pulse for ten seconds, two or three times, until sauce is a chunky puree. Chop remaining two tomatoes and add to puree. Season with salt and pepper to taste. Cover and let sit at room temperature for at least four hours.

2) Chill fontina for easier handling, and then grate.

3) Cook the pasta (add a little olive oil to the cooking water to keep pasta from sticking together) and drain. Put the pasta on a large platter, scatter the grated fontina on top, and pour the sauce over all.

Serves 4 - deliciously!

Paula Caputo

Paula Caputo

Paula Caputo danced for the New York City Ballet and was associate producer of NBC's *The Big Show* and CBS's *Baryshnikov in Hollywood.* In the Wood River Valley, Paula has graced us with her talents. She founded, produced and served as artistic director for Sun Valley Summerdance from 1988 to 1992.

I grew up back east in Toronto, and we used to tap the maple trees and make our own maple syrup in the spring. We would put syrup on everything from snow, which made "maple taffy," to toast, but this dessert was my favorite.

PaineWebber

CANUK'S CONCOCTION

Ingredients

**Fresh Pears
Plain Yogurt
Real Maple Syrup**

Slice and layer a fresh pear along with plain yogurt (preferably homemade), in a tall dessert glass. Pour REAL maple syrup on top, allowing the syrup to run down the inside of the glass.

Paul Carson

Paul Carson

After spending eight years (and achieving a third-place ranking) on the World Pro Skiing Tour, and four years on the Canadian National Ski Team, Paul chose to settle in Blaine County. Paul still remembers with glee beating Steve Mahre and Jean Claude Killy. He stays because "The mountain is the best I've skied anywhere in the world."

POLLO AI PEPERONI
Chicken with Bell Peppers

1 chicken, quartered
4 bell peppers (yellow and red), cut into
1 inch strips
8 - 10 ripe Roma tomatoes
1/2 glass dry white wine
olive oil
salt
pepper

Heat some olive oil in a deep frying pan. Add the chicken, which has been seasoned with salt and pepper. Let the chicken brown slightly - 5 minutes on each side should be enough. Add the white wine, turn the chicken again, and cook until the wine evaporates.

Place the tomatoes in boiling water for about 1 minute, then put them in the blender. Ripe Roma tomatoes are best when in season, but if you live in Sun Valley, and it's the dead of winter, use about 20 to 24 ounces (1-1/2 to 2 cans) of a good canned tomato sauce. Add the tomato sauce to the chicken and let cook, half covered, until the chicken is well done, about 1 to 1-1/2 hours.

Remove the chicken from the pan and add the bell peppers to the frying pan. Let them cook with the lid on; add water and salt if needed. When the peppers are cooked, put the chicken back into the pot and stir for about 10 minutes.

Serves 4.

Peter Cetera

Peter Cetera

For decades, Peter Cetera's angelic voice has catapulted him to the top of the charts. Hits like *The Glory of Love, Next Time I Fall* and *Even a Fool Can See* are just a few of his most recent solo coups. When not touring, Peter can be seen riding his bike faster than a speeding bullet on the bike path, or leisurely hanging out in one of Ketchum's coffee houses. The apple of Peter's eye is Claire, his angelic-looking daughter.

The Christiania Restaurant

Christine F. Bender – Prop.

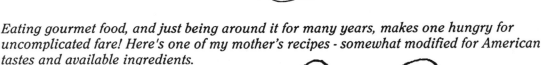

Eating gourmet food, and just being around it for many years, makes one hungry for uncomplicated fare! Here's one of my mother's recipes - somewhat modified for American tastes and available ingredients.

Chris's Austrian Meatloaf Serves 6 - 8

- 2 lbs. ground beef
- 1 lb. ground pork
- 2 cups herbed stuffing mix (I use Pepperidge Farm)
- 2 eggs
- 1 cup milk
- 3 large carrots - no need to peel them
- 2 large onions - quartered
- A pinch of each: salt, pepper, thyme, marjoram
- 2 cups beef broth, or consomme (canned is fine)
- 1 cup dry white wine

Preparation

In a large bowl, mix eggs, milk, stuffing mix, herbs, salt and pepper.
Let stand for 15 minutes to soften stuffing.
In a food processor, chop onions and carrots to medium fineness.
Add meat and 1 cup of onion/carrot mixture to stuffing in bowl, and mix well.
Put in a baking dish, molding into a loaf shape (don't use a loaf pan).
Place in a preheated 400 degree oven.
Check after 20 minutes to see if it has browned. Carefully pour off excess fat, then add remaining carrots and onions, distributing evenly around meat.
Reduce temperature to 375 degrees. When vegetables are nicely browned, add broth and wine. Bake for 1 1/2 hours.
Before serving, strain sauce into a small saucepan, pressing down on the veg etables. (My dog loves to have the vegetables mixed in with his dogfood!)
Slightly thicken the sauce with a cold water and flour mixture; simmer for a few minutes.
Adjust seasoning to taste - a hint: adding just a pinch of curry powder rounds out the flavor of any sauce!
In our house, we serve fluffy homemade mashed potatoes and a green vegetable with this hearty fall or winter dinner.

Box 3180 ♣ 303 Walnut Ave. ♣ Ketchum, Idaho 83340 ♣ (208) 726-3388 ♣ Fax 726-2530

The Christiania Restaurant

For almost as long as there has been a Sun Valley, there has been a Christiania Restaurant. In the early 30s, the "Christi" was a very posh gambling club. It is rumored that the original owner, Dutch Weinbrenner, had mob connections to Detroit's famous "Purple Gang." Owner Christine Bender, who has no mob connections, has been serving delicious meals in this historic landmark building for more than 20 years.

ENIGMA FILMS LIMITED

Pinewood Studios, Pinewood Road, Iver, Bucks SL0 0NH. Tel: 0753 630555. Fax: 0753 630393. Telex: 849577 Enigma G.

BRUSCHETTA

8 ripe Italian plum tomatoes	1 French baguette or Italian long loaf
handful of fresh basil leaves	1 pinch of dried oregano
1 tbsp. best quality olive oil	several pinches garlic powder
additional olive oil for bread	salt and pepper to taste

Yield: 4 first course portions or 24-32 hors d'oeuvres

The tomato mixture: Seed tomatoes as best you can. Chop into a fine, even dice. Mince basil leaves, or slice leaves into long thin strips. Combine tomatoes and basil in a non-metallic bowl. Add 1 tbsp. of olive oil. Add a pinch or two of oregano. Add salt and freshly ground pepper. Combine ingredients well and put aside to marinate.

The bread: Slice baguette into four even sections. Each section will roughly be the size you would cut for a sandwich. Slice the sections lengthwise from end to end. This will give you two long halves for each section. Take all 8 halves of bread and toast them, either in the broiler or individually in the toaster.

Distribute about 1 tbsp. of olive oil on a large flat plate. Sprinkle the oil evenly with garlic powder. Take a toasted piece of bread and dredge it lightly face down in the oil mixture. Do this just to coat one side of the bread. You'll need to add more olive oil and garlic powder to the plate a few times. Keep toasts warm during this process.

Assembly: Mound tomato mixture by the spoonful on each bread half, 2-3 heaping spoonfuls. Salt and then serve: As a first course, serve 2 halves on each plate garnished with fresh basil springs. As an hors d'oeuvre, cut bread into thirds or fourths before adding tomato mixture. Put on a tray and pass.

Note: Plum tomatoes are best for this recipe but 4 regular tomatoes about the size of a medium fist can be substituted. When no fresh tomatoes are available, a 14.5 oz. can of whole Italian plum tomatoes can be used, but watch the salt.

PESTO PICNIC EGGS

4 large fresh eggs	1 tbsp. pesto sauce	water

To hard boil the eggs, put whole eggs in a pot and cover generously with cold water. Put the pot on the stove and when the water boils the eggs are done. Remove the eggs from the water and let them cool, running them under cold water if necessary.

Peel the hard boiled eggs. Slice in half lengthwise. Scoop out the cooked yolks and place yolks in a small bowl. Mash pesto sauce into the yolks with a fork until it is coarsely combined.

Re-stuff egg whites with pesto/yolk mixture. Cut stuffed egg halves again lengthwise so that each whole egg yields 4 quarters. Serve. (No salt and pepper needed!)

Robert F. Colesberry

Robert F. Colesberry

Robert F. Colesberry produces feature films such as *Billy Bathgate, Come See the Paradise* and *Mississippi Burning,* that document and interpret disturbing periods in our nation's history. Two years ago, Robert was introduced to the area by his wife, Karen. Now, the Colesberrys spend as much time in Idaho as they can.

MORADA FARMS OATMEAL PANCAKES

Soak 1 cup rolled oats (quick or instant also work) in 1 cup boiling or hot tap water, with 1 tbsp. brown sugar.

Beat in 1 egg.

Add 2 heaping tbsp. plain yogurt (or 1/4 cup buttermilk)
1/2 cup milk
1/2 cup flour (white, whole wheat or a mixture of the two)
1 tsp. baking powder
1 tbsp. oil (optional)

That's it! Cook on a fiery-hot griddle. Little or no oil is needed for cooking. Serve plain, or with honey, syrup, or a mixture of seasonal fruits.

This recipe can (and should!) be adjusted according to taste and mood. Use stone-ground whole wheat flour and hearty oats for big ski days, white flour and quick oats for mellower mornings by the wood stove.

The batter looks runnier in the bowl than traditional pancake batter, but the cakes fluff up in the cooking. Also, the oats continue to absorb liquid as the batter sits, so you may want to add a little milk halfway through to maintain the light and airy texture of these fine cakes.

I can't tell you how many people this recipe feeds. My husband makes and eats the whole thing (eight or ten eight-inch cakes) almost every morning we're home. I steal a bite or two while he's making coffee, if I'm quick. Countless days of powder skiing, gate training, ski racing, rock climbing and mountain peaking have been inspired by these gentle cakes, and breakfasts at our place in the Rockies have reached legendary status among visiting friends, who even put up with a cold house and no TV in exchange for a couple of oatmeal pancakes and a cup of strong coffee.

Enjoy!

Christin Cooper

Christin Cooper

You may have seen Christin Cooper providing commentary for CBS's coverage of the 1992 Winter Olympics. Christin grew up in Ketchum "on dirt streets, exploring haunted houses and learning to love the mountains." She won a silver medal in the 1984 Olympics for giant slalom. She has the distinction of being the first and only American Triple World Championship medalist in alpine skiing.

Christopher Cord

CREAM CHEESE POUNDCAKE

Ingredients:

3 cups sugar
3 sticks butter
8 oz. cream cheese, softened
6 eggs
2 tsp. vanilla
3 cups cake flour

Directions:

Preheat oven to 300.

Cream sugar and butter. Cut cream cheese into thirds and add alternately with eggs, one at a time. Add vanilla.

Sift flour and add to mixture a cup at a time. Bake in a greased and floured tube pan for 1 hour 45 minutes. Do not use a bundt pan.

This is a large cake and quite delicious!

We received this recipe from some dear friends we met through car racing. Nancy Mandeville sent it to me in response to a recipe chain letter. Now that's a friend!

Katrina Cord

592 Warm Springs Rd., Ketchum, Idaho

Katrina and Christopher Cord

Christopher Cord won the 1987 National Driving Championship for Dan Gurney and Toyota.
His wife Katrina tells us that she was "chief cook and bottle washer for the 24-man team!"
Chris is the grandson of famous auto manufacturer E.L. Cord, who designed and sold cars in the 1930s.

BRISTOL BAY SALMON CHUNKS

2 lbs. fresh Sockeye salmon
1 large clove garlic, crushed
4 tbsp. soy sauce
1 tbsp. hot chili oil
4 tbsp. Yoshida's teriyaki sauce
2 tbsp. Wondra baking flour

Prepare the salmon by removing the skin and bones. Cut into bite-size chunks. Marinate the salmon in the teriyaki sauce, soy sauce, and garlic for about an hour.

In a large sauce pan, cook the salmon with marinade on medium heat for about twenty minutes, stirring occasionally, until the meat has cooked through.

Reduce heat; add chili oil and flour and simmer until sauce thickens.

Note: some like it hot, some like it not. Add chili oil to your own taste. Serve on a bed of steamed rice.

This is a fisherman's favorite: Fresh Sockeye salmon from the day's catch, Alaska's endless summer days, and a few fish stories over dinner.

Enjoy!

Ken Corrock

Commercial and Residential Construction • Public Works Contractor

Ken Corrock

Ken Corrock was a member of the U.S. Ski Team and a professional ski racer. Even with those impressive skiing credentials, Ken will tell you he is especially proud that in one day he skied 109,900 vertical feet on Baldy. That's more than 36 runs, or more than the average skier tackles in a week! Ken and his family have lived here since 1969.

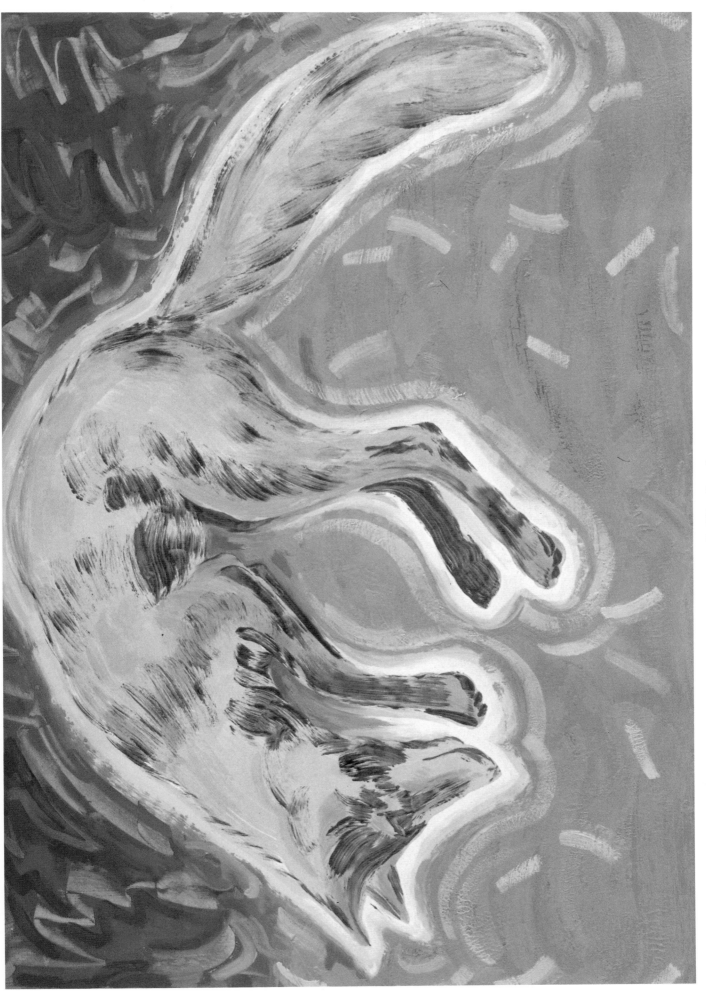

Red Fox Jumping

SHRIMP ALA HUEY

3/4 pound fresh mushrooms, sliced
1/4 cup butter
2 pounds cleaned, cooked shrimp
2 cups cooked rice, (Uncle Ben's wild-long grain)
1 cup chopped green pepper
1 cup chopped onion
1/2 cup chopped celery
1/4 cup chopped pimento
1 #2 can tomatoes, drained (2 1/2 cups)
3/4 teaspoon salt
1/2 teaspoon chili powder
1/2 cup butter, melted

Saute mushrooms in 1/4 cup butter until tender. Combine with shrimp, rice, vegetables, and seasoning. Place in greased 2 quart casserole. Pour 1/2 cup melted butter over the top. Bake in slow oven, 300' F, approximately 1 hour.

Sophie E. Craighead

This was named after Huey Long, Famous Louisiana Senator - I got this recipe in 1968 while working for Senator Mike Mansfield, D. Montana.

Sophie Engelhard Craighead

Sophie Craighead's humanitarian and political interests often cross paths. While serving as an assistant to Senate Majority Leader Mike Mansfield, she introduced the "Human-Animal Bonding Program" to the Lorton, Virginia, federal prison. This first-of-its-kind program teamed hardened prisoners with pets and decreased discipline problems there. After moving to Ketchum, Sophie became president of the Animal Shelter, and held the post for many years. She now lives with husband grizzly bear biologist, Derek Craighead, in Montana and visits Ketchum often.

SOUPED UP TURTLE BARS

Cream until light and fluffy:
1/2 cup unsalted, softened butter
1/2 cup firmly packed light brown sugar

Mix together well and add gradually to butter/sugar mixture:
1 cup flour
1/4 tsp. salt

Stir in:
1/2 cup pecans, coarsely chopped

Pat crust mixture into bottom of 9x13 inch pan. Sprinkle 1-1/2 cups pecan halves on top of crust.

Combine in a sauce pan and cook over medium heat, stirring constantly until it reaches a boil. Then boil for one minute, still stirring:
1/2 cup brown sugar
2/3 cup butter
1 tsp. vanilla, added after boiling
Drizzle over top of pecans.

Bake at 350 for 18-20 minutes or until caramel is bubbling.

Sprinkle 1-1/2 cups milk chocolate chips over top of bars and spread as they melt.

Cool completely before cutting into squares.

Elise Lufkin

90 South Hiawatha Drive • Hailey, Idaho

The Cutters of Idaho

One of only a handful of cutting facilities in the state, The Cutters of Idaho is a club offering a heated indoor arena and stalls, important in this climate, and an annual show in June. At cutting competitions, cutters (horse and rider) have two and a half minutes to choose a cow from a herd, sneak up on it and drive that cow to the center of the pen. Horses are judged on their ability to crouch and block the cow like a basketball guard blocks the offensive player.
Riders are judged on how little they use their reins and legs to guide the horse.

High Altitude Gazpacho

One 32 ounce bottle of Spicy V-8 juice
One bunch of green onions, cut into 1/4 inch slices
One head of broccoli, cut into 1/2 inch flowerets
One basket of cherry tomatoes, quartered
One large cucumber, peeled, cut in half and seeded, & cut into 1/2 slices
One yellow bell pepper, diced
One tablespoon extra-virgin olive oil
One tablespoon red wine vinegar
Two garlic cloves, minced
Two tablespoons fresh cilantro, minced

Mix all ingredients together. If desired, puree half the soup and return to original container. Chill for at least two hours. Garnish with diced avocados and serve. Bon Appétit!

This soup is great for warm summer days at Redfish Lake or late afternoon concerts at Trail Creek Cabin Grounds. Fresh baguettes or tortillas are tasty tidbits on the side.

Sherry Daech

PHONE: 208 · 726 · 3317   FAX: 208 · 726 · 0757
P.O. BOX 630, SUN VALLEY, IDAHO 83353

Sherry Daech

Driving her bright red Hummer around town like it's a compact car, Sherry Daech
is a woman on a mission. This flaxen-haired legend appears to have sold every piece of
dirt in this valley at least once. Sherry was recently seen driving her Hummer on television
screens across the country in a commercial filmed in Ketchum.

RAGOUT DI VITELLO CON TAGLIARDI
as served at Harry's Bar in Venice

PASTA

1.2 lbs. low gluten flour
5 eggs
salt
olive oil

This is all mixed together to form dough, then rested for two hours...then rolled and cut into ravioli shapes. Cook and drain. Then add olive oil, parmesan, and seasonings.

RAGOUT OF VEAL

1 litre veal stock
1-1/2 lbs. chopped
  veal rump, deboned
  (Save bones for stock.)
olive oil

Fry veal in the olive oil. Add the veal stock. (To make stock, roast the veal bones with vegetables, dump it all into a stock pot and add water. Boil and skim until there is a nice stock, adding a little tomato puree, then strain it off. The tomato puree in the stock is very important; other than that, it is basic veal stock.) Cook until veal is tender.

GREMOLADA

3 cloves garlic,
  chopped fine
Rind of one lemon,
  chopped fine
2 tbsp. basil,
  chopped fine
2 tbsp. flat parsley,
  chopped fine
1 tbsp. rosemary,
  chopped fine

Add the gremolada to the veal ragout at the last minute. Toss over cooked pasta.

John Demetre

John Demetre

Since 1964, John Demetre has reveled in Sun Valley's "beautiful light."
Throughout the years, John has designed functional and stylish athletic knitwear and ski suits
for his companies Demetre and JD Sun Valley. John is an avid pilot, golfer and skier.

MAIN STREET BOOKCAFE

Proprietors
Suzy St. Clair
Richard Dreyfuss
Steve Mitchell
Erika Mitchell
Cafe
Natalie Pruitt Judge

211 Main Street
Box 1678, Ketchum, ID 83340
208 • 726 • 3700
Fax 208 • 726 • 3726

Greek Stuffed Bread

Things to have ready:

Large mixing bowl, wooden spoon, large floured work surface, small bowl of water, 1 beaten egg, large cookie sheet sprayed with Pam and covered with corn meal, oven preheated to 400 F.

Bread:

2-2/3 cups lukewarm water
2 envelopes active dry yeast
2 tsp. sugar
6-1/2 cups bread flour
2 tsp. salt

Stuffing:

3/4 lb. feta cheese
1-1/2 cups mozzarella
1/2 cup chopped tomatoes
1 med. purple onion, sliced
20 Greek olives, pitted
2 cups steamed, dried spinach

In large mixing bowl, stir together yeast, sugar, and water. Let sit until foamy, about 5 minutes. Add 1/2 the bread flour (about 3-1/4 cups) and the salt. Mix well, until it becomes a little bubbly. The consistency should be about that of a thick batter.
Add the rest of the bread flour until you have to use your hands to knead - you can knead it in the bowl.
It should not be sticky, but not too firm to knead. Knead dough for 2 minutes.
Place the ball of dough in a bowl which has been oiled, turning to coat dough with oil. Cover with plastic wrap and place in a warm spot. Let rise for 45 minutes to an hour.
Punch down and remove dough to a large floured board. Let rest for 10 minutes.
Roll it out to form a large circle, 1/4' thick.
Spread on the herb/mayo mix*, leaving a 1/2' border all around. Evenly disperse the tomatoes, onion, feta, spinach (steamed and squeezed dry), olives, and mozzarella.
Fold the two ends together, overlapping an inch or two. Use a little water to make them stick together. Next, fold the other two sides together. The loaf will have a bit of a square shape.
Lift one end enough to slide your forearm under it. Then lift the other end until you can pick up the loaf.
Quickly flip it onto a prepared cookie sheet. Reshape to look round, being gentle so the dough doesn't tear. Coat with 1 beaten whole egg. Cut four 1/2" deep slashes into top.
Bake at 400 (or 350 in a convection oven) for 45 minutes to an hour. The loaf will feel rock hard, but it softens as it cools. Slide loaf onto a wire rack to cool.
*Herb/mayo mix: Combine 3/4 cup mayonnaise, 2 tbsp. oregano, 1 tsp. basil, 2 tsp. thyme, the juice of 1/2 lemon, and 1 clove of pressed garlic.

Richard Dreyfuss

Richard Dreyfuss is a thinking person's actor, playing a wide-range of characters on Broadway and in movies with wit and edge. Richard always knew that he would spend his life as an actor; he auditioned for his first play when he was nine. At the age of 29, he received an Academy Award for the romantic lead in the 1977 classic *The Goodbye Girl*. His roles in *American Graffiti, Jaws* and *Close Encounters of the Third Kind* mean that he starred in three of the biggest movie hits of the 1980s. Richard, an avid reader, is a partner in Ketchum's Main Street BookCafe.

D R O U G A S & C O M P A N Y
REAL ESTATE • BROKERAGE • DEVELOPMENT • CONSULTING

YaYa's Greek Dolmas with Avgolemono sauce

1-1/2 lbs. lean ground beef
1-1/2 cups long grain rice
1 onion, finely chopped
3/4 cup extra virgin olive oil
3 tbs. crushed, dried mint
1 tbs. salt
1 tbs. pepper
1 6 oz. can tomato paste

1 2 lb. jar grapeleaves
3 lemons
2 eggs

Mix first 8 ingredients. Line bottom of 3-qt pot with grapeleaves. Stuff leaves on work surface placing individual leaf vein side up, stem towards you. Place tbs. filling on leaf where stem begins. Fold bottom points of leaf over filling first, side leaves second, and roll over top point of leaf tightly. Place in bottom of pan in concentric circles, layer upon layer. Pour in enough cold water to cover dolmas. Squeeze the juice of 1 large lemon over this. Place a plate which will fit inside the pot over the dolvas so they won't unroll. Bring to slow boil and simmer about 1-1/2 hours or until rice is tender.

Avgolemono sauce: Separate eggs. Beat whites until stiff. Add yolks. Beat until blended. Beat in lemon juice just until mixed. Ladle sauce over servings of dolmas.

For a low fat version, omit ground beef and use low fat yogurt in lieu of avgolemono sauce.

Dolmas are one of my favorite Greek "soul foods" served at family gatherings at my Greek grandmother's house for as long as I can remember. They can be refrigerated and served cold with Feta cheese and Kalamata olives. Great for picnics.

Tom Drougas

220 RIVER STREET EAST, BOX 4620, KETCHUM, IDAHO 83340 U.S.A.
OFFICE 01-208-726-6000 • FAX 01-208-726-4945

Tom Drougas

Tom Drougas was an All-American football tackle at the University of Oregon, first-round NFL draft pick for the Baltimore Colts and a lineman for the Colts and the Miami Dolphins. Tom says he stays in the Wood River Valley, his home since 1975, because "the spirit of the community is tops."

DUTCHER FILM PRODUCTIONS

P.O. Box 1432
Sun Valley, ID 83353
208-726-3802

```
CEASAR SALAD DRESSING

3 large garlic cloves
1 egg yolk
1 T Dijon mustard
1 can anchovies
2 drops Tabasco
2 drops Worcestershire
1/8 cup white wine or garden herb vinegar
Juice of one lemon
3/4 cup olive oil


Mix egg yoke with mustard. Add tabasco and
worcestershire. Chop anchovies and add to mixture.
Press garlic cloves, add and mix with fork. Squeeze
in juice of one lemon and add vinegar (less than
1/8 cup according to your taste). Pour olive oil
and stir well.
```

Jim Dutcher

Jim Dutcher first caught the nation's eye in 1985 when he filmed wild beavers giving birth, a first-ever film achievement, in *Beaver Pond*. The remarkable film was shown on *National Geographic Explorer* and received national and international awards, as did a later film, *Cougar: The Ghost of the Rockies.*

37 Jim's most recent documentary, *Wolf - Return of the Legend,* was filmed for ABC's *World of Discovery.*

CLINT EASTWOOD'S SPAGHETTI WESTERN

juice of 1 lemon
12 tbsp. olive oil
12 baby artichokes
2 large cloves garlic, diced
1/4 cup finely chopped celery
1/4 cup chopped shallots
1/2 cup tomato puree
1/2 cup fish stock
salt & freshly ground pepper

1/4 tsp. thyme
1 bay leaf
2 tbsp. chopped parsley
saffron
2 tbsp. tomato paste
1/2 tsp. anchovy paste
4 clams, chopped
4 prawns or jumbo shrimp
1/2 lb. spaghetti
8 large sea scallops, quartered

12 large mussels
1/2 cup brandy
1 yellow pepper,
  thinly sliced
1 red pepper,
  thinly sliced
2 1/2 tbsp. Pernod
1/2 cup heavy cream

1. **Stir** juice from 1/2 lemon and 2 tbsp. olive oil into large pot of salted boiling water. Add artichokes and boil for 5 minutes or until almost tender. Remove artichokes and cool under cold running water. Reserve artichoke cooking water. Peel outer leaves from 8 artichokes down down to tenderest part (leave 4 artichokes with leaves intact). Cut off stem.
Cut peeled artichokes into bite-size pieces (about 1 1/2 inches long). Set aside.
2. **Add** additional salted water to leftover artichoke water, bring to a boil and cook pasta. Drain and return to pot.
3. **In a large sauté pan,** heat 7 tbsp. olive oil; sauté garlic, celery, and 2 tbsp. shallots until golden. Add tomato puree, fish stock, salt and pepper, thyme, bay leaf, parsley, 2 generous pinches saffron, tomato paste, anchovy paste and clams. Bring to a low simmer and cover.
4. **In a large sauté pan,** heat 3 tbsp. olive oil and sauté 2 tbsp. chopped shallots.
Season with black pepper. Add prawns and mussels, then cover with brandy and ignite. Remove from heat, and when flame subsides, set aside.
5. **Add** red and yellow peppers, artichokes, mussels and brandy to sauce and simmer 5 minutes. Add Pernod and cream to sauce and cook 1 minute, stirring constantly. Remove from heat.
6. **Using a slotted spoon,** remove peppers from sauce; add to spaghetti. Rinse the spaghetti/pepper mixture in hot water and drain (this is to remove traces of the sauce).
7. **Cover** the bottom of 4 flat bowls with a few tablespoons sauce. Arrange a quarter of the spaghetti in each bowl, leaving a hollow in the center. Place 2 quartered, raw scallops in the center. Arrange 3 mussels on edge of plate, and on the opposite side, place 3 artichokes. On each plate, place a reserved, uncut artichoke over the scallops. Spoon remaining sauce over scallops and mussels. Place 1 prawn in center. If preparing in advance, cover with foil and set aside. To serve, reheat in 325° oven for 20 minutes.

Clint Eastwood

Clint Eastwood's enormous talent finally received the recognition it deserved when *Unforgiven* was awarded best picture and he was awarded best director during the 1992 Academy Awards. Many years before that, however, we loved him as Dirty Harry and as an assortment of good/bad cowboys.
If you get up early enough on a deep-powder day, you can see Clint disappear into the white stuff.

STATE OF IDAHO
OFFICE OF THE ATTORNEY GENERAL
BOISE 83720-1000

LARRY ECHOHAWK
ATTORNEY GENERAL

TELEPHONE
(208) 334-2400

TELECOPIER
(208) 334-2690

SALSA
Terry EchoHawk

Roast 2 jalapeno peppers in 400 degree oven for 15-20 minutes, or until brown. (cut off stem ends)

Place in blender:
  1 lg. can whole peeled tomatoes
  1 med. onion, quartered
  1/2 tsp. dried or fresh cilantro
  1/2 tsp. garlic salt
  1 or 2 jalapeno peppers, depending on desired degree of "hotness"
  3 or 4 small tomatillas that have been boiled 15-20 min. over medium heat.
  dash of salt and pepper to taste.

Serve with chips. Refrigerate leftover salsa. (Larry loves Mexican food, especially salsa!)

COOKIE SHEET BROWNIES
Terry EchoHawk

Bring to boil in microwave:
  2 cubes margarine
  1 cup water
  4 TB. cocoa
Add:
  2 cups flour
  1 tsp soda
  2 cups sugar
  1/8 tsp salt
  1/2 cup buttermilk (or milk)
  2 eggs
  1 tsp vanilla

Pour into greased 15x20 cookie sheet with 1 inch sides. Bake 15-20 min. at 400 degrees.
FROSTING: Bring to boil in microwave: 1 cube margarine, 4TB cocoa, 6 TB buttermilk or milk. Add powdered sugar until proper consistency. Add 1 tsp vanilla and spread on brownies while warm. Nuts may be added if desired. Cut when cool.

Larry EchoHawk

As Idaho's Attorney General, Larry EchoHawk was the first Native American in U.S. history to be elected to that post. Larry, a member of the Pawnee tribe, was the 1992 recipient of the Martin Luther King Medal awarded by George Washington University. Larry, wife Terry and their six children visit Sun Valley as often as they can.

EGGPLANT PARMIGIANA

CAL NEVLAND, Chief of Police
Ketchum Police Department
Post Office Box 3008
Ketchum, Idaho 83340
(208) 726-9333

1/3 cup chopped onion
1/4 cup finely chopped celery
1 small clove garlic, minced
2 TBLspoons cooking oil
1 16 oz can tomatoes, cut up
1/3 cup tomato paste
1 bay leaf
1 tsp. dried parsley flakes
1/2 tsp. salt
1/2 tsp. dried oregano
1/2 tsp. basil
1/4 tsp. pepper
1/4 cup flour
1/4 tsp salt
1 med. eggplant, peeled and cut crosswise into 1/2 inch slices
1 beaten egg
1/4 cup cooking oil
1/3 cup grated parmesan cheese
6 ounces sliced mozzarella cheese

For tomato sauce, in saucepan cook onion, celery, and garlic in 2 Tablespoons oil
till vegetables are tender. Stir in undrained tomatoes, tomato paste, bay leaf,
parsley, 1/2 tsp. salt, oregano, basil and pepper. Bring to boiling; reduce heat.
Boil gently, uncovered, about 15 minutes or till desired consistency, stirring
occasionally. Discard bay leaf.
Conbine flour and 1/4 tsp. salt. Dip eggplant slices into beaten egg, then into
flour mixture. In large skillet brown eggplant, half at a time, in 1/4 cup hot
oil about 3 minutes on each side, adding additional cooking oil as needed.
Drain well on paper toweling.

Arrange a single layer of eggplant in bottom of 10x 6x2 inch baking dish, cutting
slices to fit. Top with half of the parmesan cheese, half of the sauce, and half
of the mozzarella cheese. Cut remaining mozzarella into triangles. Repeat
the layers of eggplant, parmesan, tomato sauce, and mozzarella. Bake, uncovered
in 400 degree oven for 15 to 20 minutes or till heated through.

6 servings

Jerry Engelbert

Jerry Engelbert

Jerry Engelbert is a four-time World Power Lifting Master champion, a former Mr. Idaho and
Mr. America and a third-place runner-up to Mr. Universe. Jerry gets plenty of respect whether
he's wearing his Ketchum Police Department uniform or working out at the gym.

Michael S. Engl

P.O. Box 2500
Sun Valley, Idaho
83353
(208)726-8151

Rotelli

with calamata olives, sun dried tomatoes, red pepper flakes and garlic

Ingredients:

rotelli pasta
Calamata olives, sliced & pitted
Sun dried tomatoes, chopped
Olive oil
Garlic
Red pepper flakes
Grated fresh Reggiano parmesan cheese

Cook pasta al dente. Add olives, sun dried tomatoes, and oil from their jar
(or add olive oil).
Chop several cloves of garlic and sprinkle on red pepper flakes.
Toss and add Reggiano parmesan to finish.

Leslie A. Engl

Leslie and Michael Engl

Michael Engl is the son of Peggy Emery Engl and Austrian Sigi Engl, who was one of
Sun Valley's most popular ski instructors and ski school directors. Through the years, the generosity of
The Engl Trust has improved the quality of life in the Wood River Valley and Idaho through its grants
to the Sun Valley Center for the Arts and Humanities, the Community School and numerous others.
Leslie Engl is on the board of the Wolf Education and Research Center.

Cristina's Prune Foccacia

DOUGH

2 1/2 tsp. yeast
1 3/4 cups warm water
3 to 4 cups flour
1 tsp. salt

Dissolve yeast in water and stir in the flour and salt. Mix, then knead for a few minutes. The dough should be soft but not sticky. Let rise, covered, for 30 to 40 minutes in a warm place.

FILLING

8 cups nice ripe plums, cut in wedges
3 cups sugar white or brown
1/4 cup olive oil
fresh rosemary (optional)

Roll half of the dough to cover the bottom of a 13-inch pie pan (about 1/2 inch thick).

Spread 5 cups of plums over the dough and sprinkle 2 cups sugar over the plums. Cover with the rest of the rolled dough. Pinch the edges, like a pie. Cover with the rest of the plums and sprinkle with the remaining sugar, olive oil and rosemary, if desired.

Bake at 350 degrees for 1 hour to 1 hour and 15 minutes, until foccacia is golden.

This recipe works well with cherries and other juicy fruit, too.

POST OFFICE BOX 5684
KETCHUM IDAHO 83340 (208)726.2717

Everett Company

Cristina Ceccatelli Cook submits this recipe in memory of Everett Halfhide, Jr.
This summertime bread was made for Cristina by her grandmother in the Italian region of Tuscany. Cristina bakes a delizioso assortment of breads, cakes and pastry at Everett Co., which opened in 1989 and serves a fresh and inspired fare.

EVERGREEN RESTAURANT
A BISTRO

Spicy Wok-Seared Shrimp
with Cappelini, Garlic, Thai Basil, Lemon Grass & Tomato

Shrimp Marinade:

1/3 cup soy sauce	1 T. honey
1 T. rice vinegar	1 T. sherry
1 T. Japanese sesame oil	5 quarter-size slices of ginger, minced
2 green onions, as thin as you can, cross cut	

Combine all ingredients. Marinate the prawns 1 - 2 hours. Drain excess marinade from shrimp. Set aside till needed.

To prep the shrimp before marinating, peel 1-1/2 pounds U16 or larger prawns. Leave the last 2 segments of shell and tail on. Slice through to that shell section, devein. This is called a fly-through.

Things to have ready for use at cooking time:

1-1/2 lbs. marinated and drained prawns
1-1/2 to 2 lbs. cappellini, dry
2 gallon pot of boiling water and a strainer
1 big hot wok or 2 large heavy saute pans
2 T. minced garlic
1/2 cup lemon grass, sliced as thin as you possibly can
1 cup very thinly sliced Thai or Italian basil, very fresh, plus 8 sprigs and a little extra for the finish
1 cup seeded and diced Roma tomatoes
2 T. red chili oil, at least, probably more if you go heavy on the pasta
Fresh parmesan, just a pinch. Shave over each dish
2 T. lemon juice

The cooking time for this should be under 5 minutes.

Fire up the wok or woks. When it's hot...
Cook the pasta in the water about 2 minutes, stirring to prevent sticking. Drain.
Put the chili oil in the wok.
Carefully add the shrimp. Try not to overload; use two woks if necessary.
When the shrimp are nearly cooked through, add the garlic and lemon grass.
Stir around. When the aromatics are well sizzled, add the basil, tomatoes and lemon juice.
Adjust for salt and oil. Add some olive oil if you don't want it spicier, chili oil if you do.
Toss pasta with the shrimp.
Divide the shrimp around the edge of the plates with tails pointed skyward, pasta in the center.
Give it a few spins. If you have more basil, sprinkle some on top with the shaved parmesan.
Garnish with basil sprigs.

Serves 4 - 8, depending on hunger level!

OFFICE: 208-726-4406 · FAX 208-726-9365 · P.O. BOX 2560 · SUN VALLEY, IDAHO 83353

Evergreen Restaurant

When Christopher and Rebecca Kastner aren't grunting up a hillside on their mountain bikes, or soaring overhead on hang gliding wings, they put their energy into Evergreen Bistro, where the cuisine soars as well. Christopher's cuisine is always a delightful surprise with influences garnered around the world, yet seeming at home when served in the bistro or in the herb garden with a bottle of wine from one of the best wine cellars in the state.

SPONGE CAKE

Ingredients:

1 3-oz. lemon Jell-O
1 cup sugar
juice of one lemon
juice of one orange
1 can Pet Evaporated milk
Graham cracker crumbs

Butter bottom of 9x13 Pyrex dish and cover with graham cracker crumbs. Set aside.

Make Jell-O with 1 cup boiling water. Stir in sugar gradually until dissolved. Add juices of lemon and orange and put in refrigerator to cool, but do not allow to set.

Whip cold Pet Evaporated milk in very cold bowl for 5 minutes. (I usually put the bowl in the freezer about 30 minutes before I need it.)

Add Jell-O gradually, while still whipping. When thick and fully mixed, pour into Pyrex dish, cover with more Graham cracker crumbs. Refrigerate.

*I can't remember when this wasn't around the house.
Because it is so light, you wouldn't believe the size of the pieces
my brother and I could eat ... and still do!*

Richard D. Bray

BARBECUE CHICKEN
WITH MUSTARD DIPPING SAUCE

Serves 6

Marinade:

1/2 cup olive oil
1/4 cup lime juice
2 cloves minced garlic
2 tbsp. chopped onion
1 tsp. Tabasco
3 lime slices

6 chicken breasts, boned and skinned

Place marinade and chicken breasts in a large bowl. Cover and place in refrigerator for 8 hours or overnight.

When ready to barbecue, remove chicken from refrigerator. Grill each side for 5 minutes.

Mustard Dipping Sauce: (1-1/4 cups)

1 cup sour cream
3 tbsp. Dijon mustard
2 tsp. Worcestershire sauce
1 tsp. lemon juice
1/2 tsp. Tabasco
1/4 tsp. pepper
2 tbsp. chopped green onion
1 minced garlic clove

Mix all ingredients thoroughly.

Good Luck !
Nancy Ferries

Famous Potatoes

Those two sunglass-sporting, lumpy potatoes are everywhere. The Famous Potato logo, sold on T-shirts and hats, has been a classic since 1979 when former Ketchum artist Julie Scott drew it for Nancy Ferries. Nancy has since developed the logo into a successful wholesale business.

Everyone eats tortillas in Spain. Torte means a round cake and the Spanish Tortilla is a round potato omelet. I chose this recipe to share with you because I think this is the real reason that my wife married me. You can serve the Spanish Tortilla as an hors d' oeuvre or a complement to dinner. It's also great for a picnic and always receives great reviews.

SPANISH TORTILLA

1/4 cup olive oil	salt	1 large onion, thinly sliced
1/4 cup salad oil	6 large eggs	6 large Idaho potatoes, peeled and cut in 1/8 inch slices

Sounds simple, but here's the real recipe. Heat the oil in a 9-inch skillet. Add potato slices slowly, alternating with onion slices, and salt each layer lightly. Cook slowly over a medium flame until tender, but not brown. In a large bowl, beat the eggs with a fork until they are slightly foamy. Salt to taste. Remove the potatoes from the skillet and drain, reserving 3 tablespoons of the oil. Add the potatoes to the beaten eggs, pressing the potatoes down so that they are covered by the egg. Let the mixture sit for 15 minutes. Heat 2 tablespoons of the reserved oil in a large skillet until very hot. Add the potato and egg mixture, spreading it out in the skillet. Lower the heat and when the potatoes begin to brown on the bottom, invert a plate of the same size over the skillet. Flip the omelet onto the plate. Add a little more oil to the skillet, then slide the omelet back into the skillet to brown on the other side. If your skillet is not hot enough, the omelet may stick to the pan. Lower the heat to medium. The tortilla should be a little juicy in the middle and hold the shape of the skillet. Transfer to a plate and let stand for 15 minutes. It is best served at room temperature. I serve this at the restaurant with a slice of Spanish Manchego cheese, a few Spanish olives, some roasted red peppers and a few slices of Spanish Chorizo. I call it Ensalada Andaluza. It may take several tries to make this a perfect round shape, but don't give up.

Felix

Felix Gonzalez

Felix at Knob Hill

Felix Gonzalez came to the Wood River Valley when he was 18 to work for Union Pacific Railroad. Thirty-two years later, he started his own restaurant, Felix at Knob Hill Inn. Felix says he developed an appreciation for savory foods as a child growing up in rural Spain. That love of food follows him to Knob Hill where he cooks in a style that is pure Felix — a blend of Mediterranean flavors, Continental know-how and Gonzalez creativity, culled from years of food experimentation.

Renee's Peanut Cole Slaw

3/4 cup plain yogurt
1 tbsp. sesame oil
1/4 cup apple cider vinegar
1/2 cup chopped red onion
1/2 tsp. cayenne pepper
1/2 tsp. pepper
1 tbsp. sugar
1 tsp. salt
3/4 cup mayonnaise
1 tsp. celery seed

1 head Savoy cabbage
1/2 head green cabbage
1/2 head red cabbage
6 grated carrots
1 cup peanuts
2 tbsp. butter

1. Blend first 10 items in blender to make dressing.

2. Shred cabbage and mix together.

3. Toast peanuts in butter (be careful - do not burn).

4. Crush peanuts and add to cabbage. Add dressing and serve immediately.

SCOTT USA
Mailing: P.O. BOX 2030 • SUN VALLEY, ID 83353   Shipping: 110 LEWIS STREET • KETCHUM, ID 83340
Phone: 208/622-1000

Administration & Marketing FAX 208/622-1005 • Customer Service (Ski/Bike) FAX 208/622-1006
Motorcycle & Pursuit FAX 208/622-1007

Chuck Ferries

Chuck Ferries was a member of the 1960 and 1964 U.S. Ski teams, and moved to
Sun Valley to start Pre Ski in 1976. Presently, he is chairman of Scott USA and Schwinn.
Chuck continues to promote skiing as director of the U.S. Ski Team.

CHICKEN HASH 'PIE'   (related to Shepherd's Pie)

Cooked white meat chicken ground or chopped
Chopped finely onion
Chopped green pepper
Chopped celery
Chopped mushrooms
Thyme
Salt
Pepper
Cumin
Can of condensed mushroom soup

Cooked mashed potatoes

Saute the onion,pepper,celery and mushrooms
Mix together in a cascerole dish the cooked ground
chicken, the cooked vegetables. Add a teaspoon of
thyme, salt and pepper to taste and a dash of cumin.
Add the can of condensed mushroom soup (do not dilute)
Stir to make sure all ingredients are incorporated in
soup.

Spread cooked mashed potatoes on top and dot with
butter.

Bake in 350° oven for half an hour to brown potatoes
on top.

Charlotte Ford

Charlotte Ford

Charlotte Ford, daughter of Henry Ford II, has been designated the "Empress of Etiquette."
Her best-selling books address modern predicaments like what to do when people use drugs in your home;
weekend guests who aren't married; even toupees, when to and when not to wear them. Charlotte is
married to Edward R. Downe, Jr. They have homes in New York, Southampton and Sun Valley.

GREATEST OLYMPIANS

Vth WINTER GAMES-1948 ST. MORITZ

© 1980 L.A. Oly. Com. ™

11

U . S . A .

GRETCHEN FRASER

Easy Pheasant

Poach two pheasants in court bouillon

Remove meat and cut into cubes.

Add 3 cans mushroom soup
and 1/4 pound grated cheese
(of your choice).

Bake at 325°
for 45 minutes.

Gretchen Fraser

Gretchen Fraser first qualified for the Olympics in 1940. But instead of ski racing, Gretchen spent those World War II years instructing amputees. Finally in 1948, the persevering skier became the first American to win an Olympic medal in skiing. When Gretchen's gold medal was stolen from the Sun Valley Lodge recently, an alarm sounded around the state for the medal, and for the beloved heroine. It was returned several months later.

Nick Maricich
and
Linda Fratianne Maricich's
Lover's Lasagna
(Sure to win his heart)

Many years ago, before Nick and Linda were married, it is told that only one thing stood between Linda and her nuptuals. Nick insisted that until she could bake him the fairest dish of lasagna, his heart would belong to Atkinson's (Ready-Made). Following is the lasagna recipe with which Linda won Nick's heart.

LOVER'S LASAGNA

1 8-oz. pkg lasagna or wide noodles	2 cups (16 oz) tomato sauce
1 cup (8-oz) creamed cottage cheese	1 tsp garlic salt
1 cup (8-oz) dairy sour cream	1/2 tsp oregano
1 tbsp. fat	Dash of pepper
1 pound ground beef	3/4 cups shredded Cheddar cheese
	1/2 cup onion

Cook noodles in boiling salted water according to package directions. Drain. Mix cottage cheese and sour cream with noodles. Brown ground beef and onion in fat. Stir in tomato sauce, garlic salt, oregano and pepper. Simmer 5 minutes. In casserole arrage alternate layers of noodle mixture and meat sauce, starting with noodles. Top with shredded cheese. Set control at 350 degrees and bake for 45 minutes. 8 Servings.

Linda Fratianne-Maricich

Linda Fratianne-Maricich

Linda Fratianne-Maricich first came to Sun Valley to skate in the ice show at the age of 15. She went on to become a two-time World Champion, four-time National Champion and 1980 Olympic Silver medalist. Nick Maricich, an incredible barrel jumper, and Linda always delight crowds at the Sun Valley Ice Shows. How many barrels can Nick jump, anyway?

Charley French
Engineer

VEGETABLE LASAGNA

2 cups sliced zucchini or chopped broccoli
1 cup sliced mushrooms
1 red sweet pepper, thinly sliced
1 medium onion, sliced
1 tomato, seeded and chopped
1 28-oz. jar spaghetti sauce or homemade
1 cup shredded mozzarella cheese (4 oz.)
1/2 cup grated Parmesan cheese
1 15-oz. carton ricotta cheese
8 oz. lasagna noodles, cooked and drained (12 noodles)
1 10-oz. pkg. frozen chopped spinach, thawed and well drained

In a large saucepan, cook zucchini or broccoli in a small amount of boiling water for 3 minutes. Add mushrooms, red pepper and onion; cook 4 minutes more. Stir in tomato. Drain well, set aside.

Reserve half of the spaghetti sauce and half of the mozzarella and Parmesan cheeses. Combine remaining mozzarella, Parmesan and ricotta cheese. Combine cooked vegetables and remaining spaghetti sauce.

Layer one-third of the noodles in a lightly greased, 3-quart rectangular baking dish. Spread with half of the cheese mixture. Top with half of the vegetable mixture and all of the spinach. Repeat layers with half of the remaining noodles and the remaining cheese and vegetable mixture. Top with remaining noodles, then reserved spaghetti sauce. Sprinkle reserved mozzarella and Parmesan cheese on top.

Bake uncovered in a 350 oven for 45 to 60 minutes or until heated through. Let stand for 10 minutes. Makes 8 servings.

You may substitute any of your favorite vegetables.

Charley French

Charley French

If you spend time outdoors at Sun Valley, chances are you'll see Charley French running, cross-country skiing or biking. Charley won the 1986 Ironman's Triathalon in Kona, Hawaii, in the 60- to 64-year-old category. He is also the 1985 National Time Trial Bicycle recordholder.

DATES F. FRYBERGER, ARCHITECT, P. A.
P.O. BOX 564
SUN VALLEY, IDAHO 83353

208 · 726 · 4207

CHOCOLATE ROLL

HAVE 5 EGGS AT ROOM TEMPERATURE

SIFT TOGETHER 3 TBSP. COCOA, 1 TBSP. CAKE FLOUR AND 1/2 CUP SUGAR.

IN A LARGE BOWL BEAT 5 EGG YOLKS. THEN BEAT IN SIFTED INGREDIENTS.

IN A SMALL BOWL BEAT 5 EGG WHITES WITH A DASH OF SALT UNTIL STIFF.

ADD 1/4 CUP SUGAR GRADUALLY. CAREFULLY FOLD WHITES INTO YOLKS.

GREASE COOKIE SHEET (10X15) GENEROUSLY, LINE WITH WAX PAPER, AND GREASE THAT GENEROUSLY.
BAKE 20 MINUTES AT 350.

TURN OUT ON TOWEL SPRINKLED WITH POWDERED SUGAR. PUT HOT WET TOWEL OVER ROLL UNTIL STEAM
STOPS; STRIP OFF PAPER. COOL ON RACK. FILL WITH WHIPPED CREAM FLAVORED WITH VANILLA OR
WALNUT COFFEE, OR FILL WITH ICE CREAM. ROLL UP.

BON APPETIT!

Dates Fryberger

Dates F. Fryberger was voted twice All American Division I hockey player, led the nation in scoring
in 1963 and played for the U.S. Olympic hockey team in Innsbruck, Austria. For Dates, playing in the
Olympic Games "fulfilled a dream as well as achieving the highest amateur honor."

BEEF BOURGUIGNON

4 lbs. lean beef or elk meat, cut into small cubes
4 T. butter
4 T. sherry
1 very large onion
15 mushrooms
2 tsp. tomato paste or ketchup
2 tsp. Kitchen Bouquet meat glaze
6 T. flour, stirred into a little consomme
2 cans consomme
2 cups red wine
salt and pepper to taste
1 bay leaf
several sprigs of thyme and marjoram (fresh or dried)
2 tsp. chopped parsley

Brown meat in butter and place in a casserole with the sherry poured over. Saute onions and mushrooms in a large fry pan. Add tomato paste, glaze, flour and consomme. Add one third of the wine; stir until boiling. Season with the salt, pepper and herbs. Cover and cook at 250 degrees for three hours. Add rest of wine as the beef cooks.

This tastes even better if made a day ahead.
Serve with rice or pasta and a good red wine.

Gardner Family

———— GARDNER RANCHES • GANNETT, IDAHO ————

The Gardner Family Ranch

Predecessors of the Gardner family crossed the plains and settled near Gannett in the 1890s. Today, Robert and Kathryn Gardner raise alfalfa, malting barley for Coors and cattle on what is one of the last originally-owned family ranch sites left in the Wood River Valley. In June, 1993, Gardner Michael Cord, the beginning of the sixth generation, was born to the ranching family.

Salmon Steak Supreme

John C. Garrett, M.D.
Keith D. Osborn, M.D.
Blane A. Woodfin, M.D.
Drew V. Miller, M.D.
Kenneth J. Kress, M.D.
Michael E. Miller, M.D.
George Cierny III, M.D.
P. Merrill White, M.D.

Makes 3-4 large servings
Light and easy
Oven Setting: 400 degrees

Ingredients

¼ cup butter
Juice of 1 lemon
1 teaspoon Worcestershire sauce
½ teaspoon salt
¼ teaspoon paprika
Pepper, freshly ground
Minced fresh parsley
About 2 lbs. salmon steaks

In a shallow pan melt the butter, add the lemon juice,
Worcestershire sauce, salt, paprika and pepper. Baste salmon with
this mixture and place steaks in pan. Bake 15 minutes or until
fish flakes with fork and is no longer translucent in the center.
Sprinkle with parsley.

The recipe presents well with asparagus and parsleyed new potatoes,
a citrus-flavored salad, and dessert.

Congratulations on
Advocates.

John C. Garrett, M.D.
Orthopaedic Surgeon
Team Physician Atlanta Falcons
Fly Fisherman,
Broncobuster Wannabee

5671 Peachtree Dunwoody Road NE, Suite 900, Atlanta, Georgia 30342 (404) 847-9999
77 Collier Road NW, Suite 2000, Atlanta, Georgia 30309   (404) 355-3344

John Garrett

John Garrett never visits Sun Valley in the fall. But it's not because he's not dying to float a Royal
Coachman fly on Silver Creek. The "Broncobuster Wannabee" and real-life orthopaedic surgeon is
too busy fixing busted-up players for the Atlanta Falcons football team. John, wife Joy and their two
daughters are up to the athletic challenge of Baldy's black diamond runs and a hike to Pioneer Cabin.

SCOTT GLENN

While Scott and I were on a film location, living in Rome, we fell in love with Penne Arrabbiata. We tried it in every restaurant we went to, and were never disappointed. When we returned home, I experimented and discovered how easy it is to make. We have not yet returned to Rome, but we are still loving our penne. We hope you enjoy it, but watch out: it's hot!

Penne Arrabbiata

The sauce:	The pasta:

1/4 cup olive oil
3 cloves garlic, minced
3 red pepper pods or
2 - 3 tbsp. crushed red pepper
3 cups plum tomatoes
2 - 4 tbsp. chopped Italian parsley
	6 qts. water
	a little salt
	1 pound penne or
	   mostaccioli (macaroni,
	   long & thin)

Heat the olive oil in a large skillet. Add garlic and crushed pepper pods; cook until golden. Add the tomatoes, crushing them as you stir. Raise the heat to a boil. Simmer for about 20 minutes, or until the tomato juice has reduced, the color has darkened, and the sauce has generally thickened.	Cook and drain the pasta. Put it onto a large platter, cover with piping hot sauce, and sprinkle with the chopped parsley.

Carol and Scott Glenn

Scott and Carol Glenn have called Ketchum "home" since 1978. During that time, Scott has played leading roles in many films including *Urban Cowboy, The Right Stuff, Silverado, The Hunt for Red October, Backdraft* and *Silence of the Lambs.* Carol Glenn is an abstract expressionistic oil and watercolor painter and exhibits her art locally and nationally.

CITRUS CHILI TOFU

THIS SPICY SAUCE KEEPS WELL IN THE REFRIGERATOR AND IS DELICIOUS ON SAUTEED OR GRILLED VEGETABLES

INGREDIENTS:
1 LB. TOFU
2 C FRESH VEGETABLES, SLICED OR CHOPPED
STEAMED RICE

SAUCE:
6 CLOVES GARLIC, FINELY CHOPPED
2 T GINGER, FINELY CHOPPED
4 T SUGAR
4 T WATER
2 T RICE WINE VINEGAR
2 T SOY SAUCE
2 T HOT CHILI PASTE
3 ORANGES, JUICED
ZEST OF 1 LIME
ZEST OF 1 ORANGE
½ RED ONION, SLICED

**USE A WOK OR CAST IRON SKILLET.
FRY TOFU AND ONION IN A LITTLE OIL.
ADD VEGETABLES AND SAUCE (TO TASTE).
COOK UNTIL VEGETABLES ARE JUST TENDER.
SERVE WITH STEAMED RICE.**

320 LEADVILLE AVE. ▲ KETCHUM, ID 83340 ▲ 208.726.1301

Globus Noodle

Globus Noodle's menu is primarily Asian with such entrees as Pad Thai and Burmese Curry. However, a diner may be surprised by dishes like Yucatan Special and Fettucini Roma. Owner, John Sweek says he developed an interest in Asian food and cooking from his grandmother Nievas, who is from the Philippines. Globus Noodle's decor is as inventive as its menu.

Tom Gorman

U.S. Olympic Men's Tennis Coach   **U.S. Davis Cup Captain/Coach**

CHICKEN VEGGIE PASTA

This is a very tasty meal, not particularly low fat, but one I would recommend the night before the Big Match. It's guaranteed to improve your second serve.

Ingredients:

1 1/4 lbs. boneless, skinless chicken breasts, cubed
12 oz. tri-color radiatore pasta (we use Ronzone)
1/2 cup chopped onion
5 medium carrots, chopped
1 medium red pepper, chopped
1 large zucchini, sliced
1/2 lb. mushrooms, sliced
3/4 cup bread crumbs, Italian style (we use Progresso)
10 oz. pesto sauce (we use Contadina)
1/2 cup pine nuts
2 tbsp. butter or olive oil
1 tsp. crushed garlic
2 tbsp. non-fat milk
1/2 cup fresh Parmesan cheese

Directions:

In a medium sauté pan, heat 1 tbsp. butter or olive oil on medium heat, adding 1 tsp. of crushed garlic. Toss cubed chicken in bread crumbs and sauté until done; set it aside.

Take a second sauté pan, add butter or olive oil and add onions. Cook until clear. Add carrots and sauté. Add red peppers and sauté. Add zucchini and sauté. Add mushrooms and sauté. Add chicken to veggie pan, stir, and keep warm on low heat.

Cook pasta per directions on box. Thin pesto with 2 tbsp. of non-fat milk. Strain pasta, pour into large bowl and mix in chicken and veggies. Pour in pesto sauce and mix well. Top with Parmesan and pine nuts.

Serve with garlic bread. Serves 4-6.

Tom Gorman

Tom Gorman

Tom Gorman, a former U.S. Olympic Men's Tennis coach, is presently the U.S. Davis Cup captain and coach and tennis director of the Ritz-Carlton Hotels. Tom, wife Danni and daughters Hailey and Kelly Ann live in Atlanta, Georgia, and spend their summers in Sun Valley.

Hearst Magazines International

George J. Green   959 Eighth Avenue   A Unit of The Hearst Corporation
President   New York NY 10019
                         212 649 2538
                         FAX 212-541-4212

"GEORGE'S FAVORITE MEAT LOAF"

```
2 pounds ground chuck
2 eggs
1 medium-sized onion, minced
2 cups fresh bread crumbs
   (4 slices white bread)
1/4 cup milk
1 teaspoon dry mustard
3/4 cup catchup
```

ABOUT 1 1/4 HOURS BEFORE SERVING:

Preheat oven to 400 F.

In a large bowl, mix ground chuck, eggs, minced onion, bread crumbs, milk, dry mustard, and 1/4 cup catchup.

In a 13" x 9" baking pan, shape the meat mixture into a 10" x 5" loaf, pressing firmly. Spread the remaining 1/2 cup catchup over top of the loaf.

Bake meat loaf 1 hour.

Makes 8 main-dish servings.
About 330 calories per serving.

Cosmopolitan • Good Housekeeping • Redbook • Esquire • Harper's Bazaar • Town & Country • Connoisseur • Countryside
Victoria • House Beautiful • Colonial Homes • Country Living • Popular Mechanics • Sports Afield • Motor Boating & Sailing
International Circulation Distributors • Eastern News Distributors • Communications Data Services
In Great Britain, The National Magazine Company Limited; Good Housekeeping • Esquire
Harpers & Queen • She • Cosmopolitan • Containerisation International Company
Antique Collector • House Beautiful • Country Living

George Green

George Green, president of Hearst Magazines International, confesses he is really a "junk food freak and eats all the wrong foods." His wife, Wilma, however, "is just about a vegetarian and · eats only the right foods." The Greens are "very happy to be part of the community," but regret "we don't get a chance to spend more time in Sun Valley."

SHRIMP BISQUE SOUP

Ingredients:

1 lb. shrimp	1-1/2 cups dry white wine
4 oz. butter	2 tsp. cooking sherry
1-1/2 c. chopped onion	1 tbsp. salt
1-1/2 c. chopped celery	1-1/2 tsp. thyme
1-1/2 c. chopped carrot	1/2 tsp. white pepper
3 cloves garlic, minced	1/2 tsp. cayenne pepper
4 c. chicken broth	1/3 cup flour
28 oz. can tomatoes in juice	3 c. half n half

Directions:

1. Melt butter in a 6-quart pot. Sauté onion, celery, carrots and garlic for 8 minutes.

2. Stir in chicken broth, tomatoes, wine, sherry and seasonings. Bring to a boil. Reduce heat and simmer, covered, for 10 minutes.

3. Stir flour into half and half and add to soup. Heat to boiling. Stir in shrimp and remove from heat.

4. Puree soup and pour it into a clean pot. Keep warm and serve, or chill and reheat.

5. Garnish with watercress sprigs and a few shrimp if desired.

Gurney's Restaurant

Gurney's, established in 1981, is a premier Hailey restaurant. Lloyd and Nancy Gurney serve an international menu in a renovated, turn-of-the-century family home on Main Street.

SOUTHERN STYLE ICED TEA

IN A MEDIUM SAUCE PAN, COMBINE:

    3 CUPS WATER
    6 TEA BAGS
    1 CUP SUGAR

STIRRING CONSTANTLY, BRING ALMOST TO A BOIL
(SHOULD BE BUBBLY).

TAKE OFF BURNER, PUT A LID ON THE PAN, AND LET SIT
FOR 25 MINUTES. REMOVE TEA BAGS.

ADD TEA MIXTURE TO 3/4 GALLON OF ICE AND WATER.

STIR.

FOR BEST RESULTS, LET SIT OVERNIGHT IN REFRIGERATOR.

Bob Hannah

Bob Hannah

Bob "Hurricane" Hannah is a seven-time national motorcross champion and three-time supercross champion. A highlight in Bob's motorcycle racing career was winning the Trophy Des Nations World Championship in 1987. Bob has two famous "back-country flying dogs," Ashley and Cally.

Dollar Mountain Mosaic

DROUGAS & COMPANY
REAL ESTATE • BROKERAGE • DEVELOPMENT • CONSULTING

Norwegian Oven Pancakes

1 teaspoon salt
4 eggs
1 quart milk
1 cube Butter
2 cups unsifted flour

Mix eggs and salt — add milk and flour
mix well

Preheat oven to 425 — melt butter in
13x9 pan first, then add mixture.
Bake 30 min.

This was one of my favorites growing up.
My mother would get up early on Sundays
and fix this filling breakfast for us before
heading up the hill for a day of skiing.

220 RIVER STREET EAST, BOX 4620, KETCHUM, IDAHO 83340 U.S.A.
OFFICE 01-208-726-6000 • FAX 01-208-726-4945

Scott Hanson

Idaho native Scott "Stork" Hanson was the 1977 World Mogul champion. He was ranked among the top three mogul skiers in the world during the 70s. Scott was a member of a 19-man, simultaneously-performed, skiing backflip, featured in the *Guinness Book of World Records*.

KIRA/H FILMS, INC.

JOSEPH HANWRIGHT
Chairman of the Board
Director - Cameraman

260 Fifth Avenue
New York, NY 10001

(212) 532-1212

CARROT CAKE

1) Sift together:
- 2 cups flour
- 2 tsp. baking powder
- 1-1/2 tsp. baking soda
- 2 tsp. cinnamon

2) Add:
- 2 cups sugar or 1 cup honey
- 3/4 cup oil
- 2 eggs
- 2 c. grated carrots (about 4 large)
- 1/2 cup chopped nuts
- 1/2 cup raisins
- 8 oz. can crushed pineapple

3) Bake in large flat baking dish about 40 -45 minutes at 350.

4) Frosting:
- 1/2 cup butter
- 8 oz. cream cheese
- 1 tbsp. vanilla
- 1 lb. powdered sugar

5) Beat all ingredients well; spread on cake.

Twenty-six years ago, I met a farmer's wife who gave me this recipe. I made it for my boyfriend, who loved it so much he married me and named his corporation after it — Carrot Cake Corp. It was a film company but everyone thought we were a bakery! Anyway, 25 years later, we're still married, a modern achievement. Maybe it'll work for you!

Patricia Hanwright

Patricia and Joseph Hanwright

Joseph and Patricia Hanwright have been making television commercials and art, respectively, from their River Run home since 1977. You've seen Joseph's electric style in Coke, Pepsi, Federal Express and Visa advertisements, and Patricia's hand in tribal-inspired, sculpted clay and jewelry in local galleries.

john & angela hemingway

CREAMY ONION AND GARLIC SOUP

8 Servings

Soup ingredients:

    10 tbsp. unsalted butter
    4 large onions, halved, thinly sliced
    6 heads of garlic
    4 tbsp. flour
    1 cup dry white wine
    6 cups beef stock or canned broth
    2 cups whipping cream or half and half
    salt and freshly ground white pepper

Crouton ingredients:

    6 tbsp. unsalted butter, room temperature
    4 ounces blue cheese, crumbled (about 1 cup)
    2 small onions, halved, thinly sliced
    4 tbsp. dry white wine
    16 1/2-inch-thick French bread baguette slices, toasted

For soup: Melt butter in heavy, large saucepan over medium heat. Add onions and garlic. Saute until tender (do not brown), stirring occasionally, about 8 minutes. Sprinkle flour over onions. Turn heat to low and cook 4 minutes, stirring constantly. Add wine and boil 2 minutes. Add stock and cream. Cook over medium heat until slightly thickened, stirring occasionally, about 20 minutes. Season with salt and pepper. (Can be prepared 1 day ahead. Cover and refrigerate.)

For croutons (essential): Using fork, blend 2 tbsp. butter with cheese in small bowl until smooth. Set aside. Melt remaining 1 tbsp. butter in heavy small skillet over medium heat. Add onion and sauté until golden brown, stirring occasionally, about 12 minutes. Add wine and cook until liquid evaporates, stirring occasionally. Transfer onion to another bowl. (Can be made one day ahead. Cover and chill cheese mixture and onion separately.)

Reheat soup over low heat if necessary. Preheat broiler. Spread toasts with cheese mixture and top with onions. Broil until cheese melts and onion heats through. Ladle soup into bowls and garnish with toasts.

Jack and Angela Hemingway

sun valley, idaho

Angela and Jack Hemingway

First son of Ernest Hemingway and father of famous daughters, John "Jack" Hemingway has led anything but a dull life. His first memories are of Paris during the 1920s with Gertrude Stein and the Idaho poet, Ezra Pound. In later years, Jack remembers skiing in Sun Valley with Ingrid Bergman, Gary Cooper and Clark Gable. The world-class angler was an OSS secret agent during World War II. When he was forced to parachute into occupied France, Jack carried the standard army gear on his back and a fly rod clutched in his right hand. Jack's book, *The Misadventures of a Fly Fisherman - And My Years With and Without Papa,* continues the Hemingway storytelling tradition.

by H₂O PLUS ™

FUSILLI WITH BASIL AND SPINACH PESTO

---

2 cups fresh basil
2 bunches fresh spinach
1/2 cup olive oil
2 cloves garlic, lightly crushed (more, if you love garlic like I do)
1 tsp. salt
1/2 cup freshly grated Parmesan cheese
1 box fusilli pasta

1. Steam spinach lightly.
2. Put steamed spinach, basil, garlic, olive oil and salt in blender or processor - blend well.
3. Cook fusilli al dente, drain
4. Mix pasta and pesto and add cheese if desired.

This is the kind of meal I like to make for my family, firstly because it's quick. My kids love pasta, and it's very healthy. (I know the family is getting their greens!)

by H₂O PLUS ™ • 676 NORTH MICHIGAN AVENUE • 39ᵀᴴ FLOOR • CHICAGO, ILLINOIS 60611 • PHONE 312 • 642-1100 • FAX 312 • 642-9207

Mariel Hemingway

Mariel Hadley Hemingway attended local schools and left Sun Valley to star in Woody Allen's movie *Manhattan,* for which she received an Oscar nomination. She has acted in 14 films and recently starred in the acclaimed television series *Civil Wars.* Mariel, Ernest Hemingway's granddaughter, exudes the kind of outdoor vitality that first attracted the writer to this area. She lists her ability to maintain a "normal, healthy family life" and a career as her greatest personal achievement.

My wife Ann and I spend as much time as we can floating Idaho rivers. This is one of our favorite Dutch oven meals. I hope you enjoy this at home or on the river.

SZECHWAN CHICKEN WITH CASHEWS

4 servings

4 skinless, boneless chicken breasts, cut in small pieces
1 egg white, beaten
1 tsp. cornstarch
1/2 tsp. salt, optional
1 tsp. finely chopped ginger root
1 tsp. soy sauce
dash of pepper

Mix above ingredients together; stir in chicken.
Cover and refrigerate at least 30 minutes.

Heat 2 tbsp. oil in 12-inch dutch oven or wok. Add chicken. Stir-fry until chicken turns white, about 3 minutes. Remove chicken from dutch oven. Heat 1 tbsp. oil in same dutch oven and add below ingredients. Stir-fry for about two minutes.

6 green onions, chopped
1 large green pepper, cut in small pieces
10 large fresh mushrooms, sliced
1 tbsp. hoisin sauce
Dried red pepper to taste (I usually start with 1/4 tsp.)

Add chicken and 3/4 cup chicken broth; heat to boiling. Mix 1 tbsp. cornstarch, soy sauce and cold water; and stir into chicken mixture. Cook and stir until thickened, about 1 minute. Stir in 1 cup cashews just before serving. Serve with white rice.

Phil Hoene

Phil Hoene

Phil Hoene played center for the Los Angeles Kings, a professional hockey team, from 1971 to 1976. He continued the hockey battle in Sun Valley, playing for the Sun Valley Suns until 1989. Recently, Phil, a graduate in Turf Grass Management, has turned his eye toward greener (if not warmer) pastures.

★ THE IDAHO ★ HIGH COUNTRY SWINGERS

Great for Mexican pot luck or for entertaining when you need something different, fast and delicious. Serve with a side salad and chips.

MEXICAN LASAGNA

1 15-oz. can chili, no beans (chili with beans is optional)
1 16-oz. jar Mexican salsa, drained (use medium or hot)
1 8-oz. can sliced mushrooms, drained
3/4 cup grated Parmesan cheese
1 1/2 tsp. fresh chopped cilantro
1 1/2 cups cottage cheese, drained
1 1/2 tsp. dried parsley flakes
9 lasagna noodles, cooked
2 1/2 cups shredded mozzarella cheese
vegetable cooking spray

Heat oven to 350°. In large bowl, combine chili, drained salsa, drained mushrooms, Parmesan cheese and cilantro. In a small bowl, stir together cottage cheese and parsley flakes. Layer noodles, cottage cheese, chili mixture and mozzarella cheese in a 9x9 baking dish coated with vegetable cooking spray; repeat to make three layers. Bake for 25 to 30 minutes or until lasagna is thoroughly heated. Let stand 10 minutes prior to serving. Serves 6 to 9.

DON'T FORGET THE MARGARITAS AND BEER.

The Idaho High Country Swingers

The Idaho High Country Swingers, a 60-member dance team, dazzles folks with their fancy stomping, swinging skirts and athletic interpretation of our Western heritage. They repeatedly win first-place trophies at regional dance contests. Swing your partner 'round!

selene bondurant isham
2 0 8 - 7 8 8 - 3 6 3 8
box 1687 ketchum, idaho 83340

A WONDERFUL BREAKFAST LAMB HASH

1 tbsp. grated horseradish
1/2 cup sour cream
1/2 tsp. fresh lemon juice
1/4 tsp. fresh ground pepper
4 medium russet potatoes, peeled,
  cut into 1/2 inch dice
1/4 cup olive oil
1 large onion, coarsely chopped
3 thick slices of bacon,
  cut into 1/2 inch dice

4 cloves garlic
2 cups cooked lamb from braised lamb shanks
1 tsp. finely chopped fresh thyme
1 tsp. finely chopped fresh marjoram
1/4 tsp. ground cumin
pinch of turmeric
salt and freshly ground pepper
1/2 cup heavy cream
4 large fresh eggs
1 tbsp. chopped fresh parsley

Combine horseradish, sour cream, lemon and pepper and let stand. Heat frying pan. Add bacon and onion until onion is translucent.

Add garlic, cook two minutes more, then add potatoes. Continue to cook over medium heat, stirring often until potatoes are three quarters cooked.

Mix in lamb, thyme, marjoram, cumin, turmeric and season with salt and pepper. Cook, stirring once or twice, until potatoes are done, about 5 minutes more.

Add the cream and turn up the heat to thicken the cream and form a light brown crust on the bottom. Flip the hash and brown on the other side.

While the hash is cooking, poach the eggs. Divide the hash on plates, put a spoonful of horseradish cream in the center of each serving and top with eggs. Sprinkle with parsley.

Selene Bondurant Isham

Selene Bondurant Isham has catered for Barbara Walters, Sylvester Stallone, Faye Dunaway, Fred Astaire and Bo Derek. She has published articles in *Sunset* and *Gourmet* magazines. Selene says it has taken her a long time to realize that food can still taste great without using butter and cream as staples.

Mrs. William C. Janss
Post Office Box 329
Sun Valley, Idaho 83353

Pear Chutney/Plum Chutney

8 cups peeled, cored and diced pears or plums
1 lb. light brown sugar or 1 cup honey
2 cups raspberry or other berry vinegar
1 large onion, chopped
1 cup raisins, dark or light
2 oz. crystalized ginger
2 large cloves garlic, minced
1½ tsp. cayenne pepper
1 tsp. salt
1 large tsp. nutmeg, allspice and cinnamon
2 tsp. mustard seed
chopped walnuts or pecans if desired

Boil vinegar and sugar briefly. Add remaining ingredients and simmer one hour.

I add honey and dried ingredients just before canning. I cooked plums alone first, then seeded, then added to mixture to cook with remaining ingredients.

Makes 8 jars, 1/2 pint each

This recipe was developed as a result of having a wonderful prune/plum orchard at my farm called "The Last Resort" outside of Salmon, Idaho. If you can find prune/plums, I highly recommend them for this recipe. One of my most meditative experiences in life was canning; I highly recommend it for relaxation and a feeling of productivity. Friends can always be the recipients then of your thoughts and efforts.

Glenn C. Janss

It is no wonder *The Los Angeles Times* named Glenn C. Janss "Woman of the Year for Arts Education." While Glenn has certainly made her mark nationwide, her devotion to art has made a significant difference in the lives of many Idahoans. She was founder of the Sun Valley Center for the Arts and Humanities, and served as its chairwoman for 15 years. The 300-piece Glenn C. Janss Collection of American Realist Drawings and Watercolors is on long-term loan to the Boise Art Museum.

William C. Janss
Post Office Box 107
Sun Valley, Idaho 83353

Steamed Quail with White Grapes

This is an old and traditional recipe.

> 4 quail
> 3 tbs. butter
> 1/4 cup strong chicken broth
> 1/4 cup dry white wine
> 2 ozs. Armagnac
> 1 cup seedless grapes
> 4 slices toast
> salt and freshly ground pepper

First: Melt the butter in a skillet and brown the quail on all sides. Season them with salt and pepper and add the broth and the wine. Cover the pan and simmer gently for about 10 minutes.

Second: Remove the cover, pour warmed Armagnac over the quail and ignite it. Add the grapes, cover the pan, and continue simmering for a few minutes, or until the birds are well done.

Third: Place each quail on a toasted bread slice or on liver toast and pour the pan juices and grapes over them.

Serves 2.

P.S. This applies to other game; i.e., dove, partridge and even rock cornish hens.

William C. Janss

For many baby boomers, the name Janss means Sun Valley. William C. Janss owned the resort from 1968 to 1977. There are enough experiences listed in Bill's resume to fill several lifetimes: U.S. Ski Hall of Fame inductee, director of Head Ski Corp., founder and developer of Snowmass Ski Area, Beverly Hills developer, cattleman, director of winter sports for Yosemite National Park, pilot for U.S. Air Corp., member of the U.S. Olympic ski team and three-year letterman for the Stanford ski team.

DONNA KARAN

NEW YORK
BITT'S PIZZA

Preheat pizza stone or tile for 1 hour at highest oven temperature.

BITT'S PIZZA DOUGH

Yields: 19 single-serving (12") pizzas

INGREDIENTS
1 quart warm water
1/2 oz. Eagle yeast
2 oz. extra virgin olive oil
3 1/2 lbs. All Trumps High-Gluten Bread Flour
2 tbsp. salt

DIRECTIONS
Place water in mixing bowl. Dissolve yeast in 1/2 cup water. Add to bowl. Add oil, then flour. Knead for 5 minutes, add salt, continue kneading for 10 minutes. Remove dough, place in oiled bowl and cover with plastic wrap. Let rise for 1 hour then cut into 4 1/2 oz pieces and roll.

BITT'S PIZZA TOPPING

Yields: 1 (12") pizza

INGREDIENTS
1 cup arugula
3 chopped cloved roasted garlic
1/4 cup chopped roasted onion
1/2 cup diced roasted red and yellow pepper
4 tbsp. chopped pitted black olives
4 oz. crumbled fresh goat cheese
1 oz. lemon vinaigrette (see below)
Salt and pepper to taste

DIRECTIONS
Roll pizza shell and brush with oil. Bake until crispy golden then pierce air pockets with toothpicks. Place in bowl arugula, peppers, garlic, onions, olives, salt and pepper. Mix in vinaigrette, stir well. Place mixture on baked pizza shell and top with goat cheese.

LEMON VINAIGRETTE

Whisk together 2 tbsp. fresh squeezed lemon juice and 5 tbsp extra virgin olive oil.

THE DONNA KARAN COMPANY
550 SEVENTH AVENUE NEW YORK CITY 10018 TEL 212-789-1500 FAX 212-764-4396

Donna Karan

From sport socks to silk suits, DKNY and her signature line Donna Karan are bought in urbane boutiques and chic Old West restorations, like Ketchum's Mercantile. Donna spends holidays in Sun Valley when she can get away from the frenetic fashion world.

JANET KELLAM

SALMON RIVER SEED BREAD

5 1/2 cups warm water
4 tbsp. dry yeast
2 tsp. salt
2/3 cup molasses
1/2 cup oil
1 egg
1 egg beaten with 1 tbsp. water for glaze
6-7 cups whole wheat flour
6-7 cups white flour

4 tbsp each:
poppy seed
flax seed
sesame seed
sunflower seed
pumpkin seed
millet

Combine water and yeast, let proof 3-5 minutes.
Combine all liquid ingredients and add yeast mixture (save 1 egg for glaze)
Add half the amount of flours and mix to batter consistency.
Let sit 20-60 minutes in a bowl covered with a towel.
Add remaining flour and knead until it's of dough consistency.
No need to wait for dough to rise; simply form round loaves and place on an oiled cookie sheet.
Slash tops 3-4 times with knife, and brush loaves with beaten egg.
Place in 350° oven (doesn't need to be preheated) and let bake 30 minutes to an hour. Time depends on size of loaves, preheat or not, and how closely spaced.
Loaves are done when tapping on bottom produces hollow sound.

There's nothing that gives that comforting feeling of home more than freshly baked bread. I shared this favorite recipe with the cook on our sailboat in Antarctica. We would return from long cold days on the water in the little Zodiacs, rounding the last iceberg home, to be welcomed by the aroma of warm bread. Many tales were shared around the galley table over a loaf or two of this!

Advocates have gone far beyond the smell of warm bread in helping survivors of domestic violence re-establish a true home in their lives. Here's wishing them much success and support in their work.

P.O. Box 3572
110 Board Loop
Ketchum, ID 83340
(208) 726-1640

Janet Kellam

As a sound recordist, Janet Kellam captured the icy score of the last frontier, Antarctica, for the National Geographic Explorer documentary *Journey to the Bottom of the World.* Closer to home, Janet is currently working on an Audubon/Disney program titled *Going Home to Yellowstone.*

Dog Bits

Ingredients:

8 cups whole wheat flour
2 tbsp. molasses
2 tbsp. honey
approx. 2-1/2 cups warm water
2 tbsp. safflower oil

Directions:

Warm the flour in oven for about 1 minute, until warm.
Make well in middle of flour.
Pour molasses, honey and water into well.
Mix to a sticky dough.
Cover and let sit for 15 minutes.
Make another well and add oil to the middle of it.
Mix well.
Shape into balls.
Bake 35-40 minutes at 375.

April's dumpster tour of Ketchum · First stop is Chez Michel for hors d'oeuvres, then up Leadville Avenue to Louie's for some pasta (remembering to look both ways before crossing the street). It's worth the hike over to the Christiania for the possibility of lamb shanks · my favorite entree · and then I waddle up the street to Ketchum Grill for a salad (ever· mindful of the Police station; there IS a leash law here, you know!). After dessert at Piccolo's, I toddle home to bed with a full tummy.

Ketchum Canines

This recipe is from all those hard working dogs of Ketchum. You've seen them in book stores, the post office and helping the Ski Patrol on Baldy. We're sure that per capita, there are more dogs drooling from the backs of pickups in Ketchum than anywhere else in the nation.
Thanks to April "Bookhound" Demetre for the translation.

K E T C H U M

Scott W. Mason
Managing Partner/Chef

Savory Roquefort Cheesecake

Sometimes on the way to and from work my mind wanders. Cheesecake, the sweet kind, was on my mind the day I came up with this savory cheesecake. This recipe has become the most requested recipe at the Ketchum Grill.

Crust: 3 cups finely chopped almonds
            4 Tablespoons unsalted butter, melted
            2 Tablespoons honey

Filling: 1-1/4 pounds cream cheese
            2 eggs
            2 Tablespoons port wine
            1/2 pound french Roquefort cheese
            Large pinch white pepper

Mix almonds, melted butter and honey together. Press into the bottom and sides of an 8" springform pan with the back of a spoon. Bake at 400° for 10 minutes.

In a mixer or processor, mix cream cheese until smooth. Add 2 eggs, mix. Add port wine and white pepper, mix until smooth. Fold in crumbled Roquefort cheese. Spread in to crust-lined springform pan. Bake at 325°-350° until light brown on top (approximately 45 minutes to 1 hour). Allow to cool before cutting. Serve with a salad of watercress or baby lettuces and a light raspberry vinaigrette.

Makes 10-12 slices.

Scott Mason

520 East Avenue Ketchum, Idaho 726-4660

G R I L L

Ketchum Grill

In 1991, Scott and Anne Mason realized a piece of their dream when they helped start Ketchum Grill. It's located in the historic Ed Williams' home, a circa-1885 bungalow built by Ketchum's first postmaster. Anne creates the restaurant's tempting desserts and breads. Scott orchestrates the rest . . . from smoking meats at home, to collecting forest morels and watercress, to combining a myriad of fresh ingredients in flavorful and unusual dishes.

ALISON OWEN KIESEL

Box 2234
Ketchum, ID
83340
208.726.9243

BASQUE SHEEPHERDER BREAD

1/2 cup oil
1/2 cup sugar
1 1/2 tsp. salt
2 pkg. dry yeast
9 1/2 cups flour

Combine oil, sugar, salt and 3 cups hot water in a bowl. Stir and let cool to lukewarm. Stir in yeast. Let stand for 15 minutes or until bubbly. Add 5 cups flour; beat well. Add remaining flour; mix well. Knead on floured surface until smooth and elastic. Place the dough in a greased bowl, turning to coat surface.

Let rise until doubled in bulk. Punch dough down. Place in greased medium-sized dutch oven. Cover with greased lid. Let rise until lid lifts slightly. Bake covered, at 375° for 12 minutes. Bake, uncovered, for 30 minutes or until bread tests done.

(Note: I have found that the bread takes an extra 15 minutes baking time at this altitude. Also, I put the bread in the oven just before the lid lifts, because it continues to rise in the oven.)

P.S.: This is a fun item for potlucks and parties!

Alison Owen Kiesel

Alison Owen Kiesel is a pioneer. She was the first woman to race in the U. S. Nordic Junior Nationals, and the first and only American woman to win a Nordic Cup World Race. Alison has skied in two Olympics. She has two children and coaches the Sun Valley Ski Education Foundation Nordic ski team.

CAROLE KING

KITCHEN SINK SALAD
(No salt/no oil)

1 medium head romaine lettuce
2-3 stalks celery, including leaves
2 tomatoes
6 radishes
1 clove garlic
1 large basil leaf, chopped, or 1/2 tsp. dried basil
1/4 cup-1/2 cup grated Parmesan cheese, to taste
1 green pepper or 6 cherry peppers (red or green)
1 carrot
6 mint leaves, chopped, or 1/2 tsp. dried mint
juice of 2 small lemons
Optional:
one apple, diced
1 raw beet, grated
1/4 cup nuts or sunflower seeds
1/4 cup sprouts
croutons
anything else except kitchen sink

Rub a clove of garlic over the inside of a large salad bowl. Tear lettuce, cut vegetables into bite-size pieces and put into bowl. Add optional ingredients, if desired. Add the basil, mint, lemon juice, and Parmesan cheese. Toss well and serve.

Makes 6 servings!

Carole King

Carole King

Songs from the album *Tapestry* are imprinted into the minds of most baby-boomers, and it's not surprising since four of its twelve songs scaled the charts to number one. Carole's singing successes are well known, although not everyone knows that she also wrote such songs as *You've Got A Friend* and *The Locomotion,* recorded by stars like James Taylor, Ella Fitzgerald and Grand Funk Railroad. Carole, who owns a ranch north of Sun Valley in the Idaho wilderness, was inducted into the Rock and Roll Hall of Fame.

SMOKED CHICKEN & PASTA
A LA FISHER CREEK

To smoke chicken, using the whole chicken, discard the giblets. Wash and fill cavity with a quartered orange (orange will be discarded later). We use a Webber grill but a gas one is okay. Place charcoals and pieces of wood as large as your grill will accommodate. Set a pan filled with water on the grill and put a smaller grill on top of the water pan. Place chicken on top of water grill and cover loosely with foil. Cover the grill and open holes only enough to keep the fire from smothering and sustain a moderate temperature. (A large chicken takes about 4 hours up here. I'm at 7,000 feet, at the foot of the Sawtooth Mountains in central Idaho.) When the chicken is done, cool it enough to remove meat with your fingers. I usually cook 2 chickens and freeze what I don't use.

Since I never measure ingredients, the following is a guide. As a painter, I've just never responded well to directions, particularly when they are printed.

Serves approximately 6

1. In a saucepan, put in about 2/3 cup plain yogurt, 1/2 container of fat free Philly cheese, 1/2 cup no-cholesterol mayonnaise.

2. Coarsely chop about 1/3 cup <u>fresh</u> basil, 1 tsp. Dijon mustard, 1 tsp. orange juice concentrate, if it's handy, 2/3 tsp. green peppercorns, salt to taste.

3. Heat, but don't boil (boiling fat free Philly does peculiar things when it gets too hot).

4. Cook spaghetti or angel hair pasta.

To serve, put a generous portion of smoked chicken on top of spaghetti, spoon on sauce and garnish with an orange slice and a sprig of basil.

Alternatives - These are important, because doing this the same way every time just isn't fun. So, I alternate with various items just for the hell of it. The list follows: **dried tomatoes,** a few ounces of **scotch** (alcohol burns off, but flavor is robust with smoked chicken), chopped **jalapeno** peppers or some **garlic,** <u>fresh</u> **savory** or **rosemary,** strips of **red pepper** braised in olive oil (very good).

This is a robust meal and great when served with Caesar salad and some fruit for dessert.

Joseph Kinnebrew

The Guggenheim Museum, Metropolitan Museum of Art, and Library of Congress collections include Joe Kinnebrew's art. Joe was invited to participate in the State of the Art '93, the largest and most competitive juried exhibition in the United States.

Damaris D. W. Ethridge
Proprietor

I prepare this wonderful recipe for my friends who come over for dinner in Idaho. If I'm lucky enough, my husband, Bill, and I will catch the fish that day! Please enjoy cooking the trout in this recipe. Of course, I serve my prize wine, the Landmark Damaris Reserve, to top it off!

POACHED TROUT

6 trout, whole and boned
2 onions, thinly sliced
9 tbsp. butter
1 cup Chardonnay
1 cup broth

salt and pepper to taste
1 bay leaf
2 garlic cloves, crushed
1/2 cup bread crumbs

Serves 6

1. Sauté the onions in 3 tbsp. of butter until they are soft.

2. Add the chardonnay, water, broth, salt, pepper, bay leaf and garlic. Bring to a boil and cook for 10 minutes.

3. Add trout to the pan and reduce heat to simmer. Poach for at least 10 minutes, basting often.

4. Sauté the bread crumbs in the remaining butter until they are brown.

5. Arrange the trout on a platter. Pour 1 tbsp. poaching liquid over each fish, then distribute the butter and bread crumbs on top.

Damans Ethridge

LANDMARK VINEYARDS

249 Royal Palm Way
Suite 403
Palm Beach, Florida 33480
(407) 835-8355
FAX (407) 835-8009

Landmark Vineyards

California's Landmark Vineyards owner and Sun Valley resident Damaris D.W. Ethridge started Flying Doctors of Africa and has served on many hospital boards, including Stanford's, and on the board of Conservation International. Damaris said she inherited a social conscience from her great-great grandfather John Deere.

Nicki Lee

TO - DIE - FOR - POTATO SALAD

5 lbs	New (Red) Potatoes, cooked, peeled and diced into small cubes
1 large	Red Onion diced small
10	Hard Boiled Eggs diced
1 lb	Bacon (crisp) chopped

DRESSING:

6 cups	Best Foods Mayonnaise
1 pint	Sour Cream
1 1/2 tbs	Lemon Juice
To Taste	Salt and Pepper

Serves: A good size party!

Combine the dressing ingredients -
Once the potatoes, eggs and bacon are cool combine with the onion and add about 3/4 of the dressing, mixing well. Refrigerate for several hours along with remaining dressing. Before serving mix in remaining dressing - salad should be quite moist.
This also makes a dynamite macaroni salad

My mother and I have collaborated on t his salad and it has always been a big hit!

Nicki Lee

Nicki Lee, only child of singer Peggy Lee and guitarist Dave Barbour, has lived in Sun Valley since 1973. Nicki has owned and operated an art gallery, directed children's theatre workshops and performed in community theatre productions. One of Nicki's botanical pen and ink drawings encircles this recipe.

RATATOUILLE

Ingredients:

2 small or 1 medium eggplant, peeled and diced
1 large onion, chopped
2 green peppers, thinly sliced
2 medium or 4 small zucchini, sliced
1 large or 2 small cans whole tomatoes
2-3 large cloves garlic, crushed
1 tbsp. sugar
1 tbsp. white wine vinegar
1/8 tsp. basil
1/8 tsp. oregano
salt and pepper to taste
olive oil
Mr. & Mrs. T or Spicy V-8 juice
yellow squash, diced (optional for added color)
pitted olives (about 25 or 1 small can)

Place all ingredients except olives in a large Dutch oven.
Sprinkle with at least 5 tbsp. olive oil and, at least, 1 cup
Mr. & Mrs. T or spicy V-8. Cover and cook slowly in 300-325°
oven for about 1 hour or until eggplant and zucchini tender.
Top with olives before serving (if desired).

Ruth Lieder

Telephone 208-622-4438 • P.O. Box 416 • Sun Valley, Idaho 83353 • FAX 208-622-3401

Ruth Lieder

Sun Valley Mayor Ruth Lieder is known locally for astute city management,
performing high-altitude weddings on Bald Mountain and carting around a station
wagon packed with Golden Retrievers. Nationally, Ruth is known as a former reporter
for *Sports Illustrated* and marketing manager for *Asia Magazine*.

Potato Squash Soup

1.5	pounds golden finnish potatos
1.7	pounds summer squash
2	cans 16 oz chicken broth
3	tablespoons fresh dill weed
3	tablespoons butter
	salt & pepper to taste

Wash (don't peel) potatos and squash. Chop
into 2 inch size pieces. Put in pan and cover
with the chicken broth. Add water, if needed,
to cover the vegetables. Bring to a boil, then
simmer for 20 minutes. Chop the dill weed,
and add along with the salt, pepper, and butter.
Simmer for another 20 minutes. Mash with large
fork or masher, or puree.

L. Maria Maricich DC

L. Maria Maricich

Sun Valley native L. Maria Maricich was a six-year member of the U.S. Ski Team
and skied on the 1984 Olympic team. Maria now practices chiropractic healing in Ketchum
where she keeps prospective Olympians and the rest of us flexible and healthy.

SPICY SESAME NOODLES

1 lb. Asian or regular noodles
1/3 cup peanut butter
1/2 cup water
3/4 lb. firm tofu (mashed or cubed)
1/4 cup dry sherry or mirin
6 tbsp. soy sauce
4 tbsp. sesame oil
1 tbsp. honey or sugar
3 tbsp. sesame seeds
1/2 tsp. cayenne
1 cucumber, sliced
4 green onions, sliced

Cook noodles according to directions. Stir peanut butter and water over low heat. Add next 7 ingredients and stir. Drain noodles and toss with sauce. Sprinkle green onions and cucumber over the top and serve.

Pamela Sue Martin

Pamela Sue Martin

Pamela Sue Martin happily traded playing Dynasty's glamorous, troubled and tempestuous Fallon for a role as a mom living a quiet life in Hailey. She exits from that real-life role for short periods to pursue theatre and television projects. Pamela Sue began her acting career with a seven-year stint as Nancy Drew on the 1960s television series of the same name.

Wendall McCall
110 Hurst Lane – Bellevue, Jdaho 83313

KLICK'S UNFLAPPABLE
SALMON RIVER FILLETS

Note: Chris Klick is one of the only book characters, who, when river guiding the Owyhee, takes a solar-powered microwave along with him, just so he can prepare this dish to perfection. For those faint of heart of running electrical devices near water, you can skip the microwave, but in that case, the fish should be more slowly cooked (covered barbecue works), not quite as hot for four to seven minutes before placing fillet directly over coals. Either way, the idea is to get the center of the fish cooking before it hits the hot stuff!

Fish: approx. 1 to 1-1/2 lbs. fillet
1/2 cup tamari (or soy) sauce
1/4 cup rice vinegar

Remove scales with knife - taking note not to remove your finger, too - wash fillet thoroughly in cold water; marinate in two parts Tamari (or soy sauce) with 1 part rice vinegar for 1-2 hours before cooking.

A few minutes prior to barbecuing, microwave fillet for 2 to 3 minutes on high, rotating (not flipping) once.

Barbecue over hot coals, meat side down, for 4 to 5 minutes; flip (with two spatulas) onto skin, cook another 3 to 5 minutes. Check center with fork - meat should be moist and a deep pink inside. If extremely artful with a spatula, you can now divorce the fish from its skin which will stick to the grill, the fat allowing it to separate, as it heads to the platter.

Yum. Break camp
and head down river.
Catch some trout.
Try with the trout as well.
After all, you brought all that marinade!

Wendall McCall

Wendall McCall made his living as a bass player and rodeo rider for twelve years before taking to writing mysteries. He has also laid fence, been a river guide, and a brick mason. He is presently preparing to marry his fourth wife, LeAnn Chambers. He is kept company by his dog, Scout, and divides his time between Bellevue and the Barking Bear Ranch in Challis. He is the author of *Dead Aim, Aim For the Heart* and *Concerto in Dead Flat*, due in 1994.

BANANA BURRITO

This is a simple meal I devised while in Kona, Hawaii,
training for my first Ironman Race in 1980.

Ingredients:

1 ripe banana
1 whole wheat tortilla

Directions:

Wrap banana in tortilla and it's ready. Fits easy in pocket of bike jersey.

Optional extras: peanut butter, almond butter, healthy jams and jellies*

*Not advisable in jersey pocket.

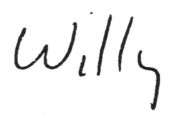

▼

SHOESTRING
INCORPORATED
208-726-7533

P.O. BOX 2311
KETCHUM, IDAHO
83340

TOLL-FREE
1-800-999-2342
FAX 1-208-726-3952

Willy McCarty

An athletic trainer since 1977, Willy McCarty has spurred stars like Cher and Bette Midler
and local couch potatoes into shape with "a philosophy of fun, love of exercise and training easy." Willie
has taken fourth-place in the Ultra-Man contest, a 150-mile bike ride, two-marathon run and six-mile
ocean swim. While training for Hawaii's Ironman, Willy invented "Easy Laces," a lockable elastic shoe-
lace. They are perfect for extreme athletic events because you never have to tie or untie your shoes.

The Wood River Journal

· S E R V I N G   B L A I N E   C O U N T Y   S I N C E   1 8 8 1 ·

BARBARA'S STRAWBERRY SILK DESSERT

Crumb Mixture
1 cup sifted flour
1/4 cup light brown sugar
1/4 cup chopped pecans
1/2 cup melted butter

Combine all ingredients to create a crumb mixture. Scatter in a 9x13x2 inch deep pan. Bake at 350° for 20 minutes or until lightly browned, stirring occasionally. Let the crumbs cool while you are mixing the remainder of the ingredients.

Fruit Mixture
2 egg whites
2 cups (firm packed)
  sliced strawberries
1 cup white sugar
2 tbsp. fresh lemon juice
1 cup cream

Beat egg whites, strawberries, sugar and lemon juice with electric mixer until thickened, about 10 minutes. Whip one cup of cream and add it to the berry mixture.

Put 2/3 of the cooled crumb mixture in the bottom of the 9x13x2 inch pan. Spread strawberry mixture evenly on top, then cover and freeze. If making for same-day use, this needs about 6 hours to freeze solidly.

At serving time, take the dessert out of the freezer about 20 minutes before you will be cutting it. Top with remainder of crumbs. Cut into squares and place fresh berry atop each serving.

Roberta McKercher

Post Office Box 988   Hailey, Idaho 83333   (208) 788-3444 or 726-8231   Fax: (208) 788-0083 or 726-2634

Roberta McKercher

Roberta McKercher could have received her literary muse from Ezra Pound's ghost. Her Hailey home is the famous poet's birthplace. Roberta has been writing for the *Wood River Journal* for more than 50 years. She is well-known for her work with the Little League, Boy Scouts and Jobs Daughters. The City of Hailey's gateway park is named in her honor.

MOTHER ANN'S MOLASSES COOKIES

1 cup each brown sugar, buttermilk, Grandma's Molasses
1 egg
2 heaping tsp. soda, dissolved in buttermilk and molasses
1 tsp. ginger
1/3 tsp. cloves
1 tsp. allspice
1 tsp. cinnamon
1/2 tsp. nutmeg
5 cups flour
2 sticks margarine, melted
1 1/2 tsp. salt

Mix all ingredients together in a large mixing bowl, and drop by tablespoons onto an ungreased cookie sheet.

Cook at 350° for 14 minutes at Sun Valley's altitude, 10 minutes at sea level.

ICING

1 lb. powdered sugar
1 stick margarine

evaporated milk
vanilla to taste

Cream the margarine into the sugar and add enough canned evaporated milk (a few ounces) to make icing spread well. Flavor with vanilla and a pinch of salt, and beat until fluffy. Let cookies cool before frosting.

Makes 4-5 dozen cookies.

Passed along the McKinley side of my family for generations, from farm stock to the McKinley White House, these cookies are the instant target of visitors to my mother's home. Mildred McKinley McMahan, born in 1901, welcomes her family, from great-great-grandchildren to her wanton post-pubescent snow boarding son, with the aroma of these great cookies. I hope other families will enjoy this recipe, too.

P.O. BOX 2357 SUN VALLEY, IDAHO 83353 208 726-9022

Bill McMahan

At the age of 49, Bill McMahan competed in the "Legends" category at the 1993 U.S. National Snowboarding Competition. Bill endured his first boarding days with "massive doses of anti-inflammatories." His snowboarding diet includes "polish sausage, ice cream and fish & chips."

Middle Fork Wilderness Outfitters receives many requests for recipes after a week on the river, but Chicken Sales gets the most votes. Named after the guide that helped develop it and who swears he makes it better than anyone, we make this in a 12" Dutch oven and bake with hot coals (about 12 on the lid and 5-6 underneath). If adapting to oven baking, use a heavy casserole with lid. Serves 15.

CHICKEN SALES

1 1/2 lbs mushrooms, sliced
1/2 lb peppered bacon, chopped
6 shallots, chopped
1/4 cup olive oil
1/2 lb butter
1 cup vermouth or dry white wine
6 oz tarragon vinegar

2 tsp. dry Italian herbs
8 oz mozzarella cheese, shredded
1/2 cup parsley, chopped
3 large tomatoes, chopped
15 boneless skinless chicken breasts
Flour

-Flour chicken breasts and brown in large skillet using a mix of butter and olive oil to keep from sticking. Transfer to large baking dish, or Dutch oven, coated with cooking spray.
-Saute mushrooms and shallots, adding as much olive oil and butter as necessary. Add bacon and cook until bacon is done. Pour tarragon vinegar over all. Sprinkle mixture with flour and add vermouth until a sauce consistency is formed. Stir in Italian herbs.
-Spoon mixture over chicken breasts and sprinkle with mozzarella cheese.
-Cover and bake at 350 degrees for 30-40 minutes. If using a Dutch oven, it is okay to peek but do not completely lift the lid.
-Remove from oven at end of baking time or lift lid of Dutch, sprinkle with chopped tomatoes and parsley. Cover and return to oven for 5 minutes.

We serve this accompanied by linguini with pesto sauce, fresh asparagus, Caesar salad, a good Chardonnay, and lemon cheesecake with huckleberry topping for dessert. This is an especially fine meal when sitting in a comfortable chair in the middle of the wilderness watching the moon rise and listening to the rush of the river.

Middle Fork Wilderness Outfitters

P.O. Box 575 • Ketchum, Idaho 83340 • 208 / 726-5999

Recycled ♻

Middle Fork Wilderness Outfitters

Middle Fork Wilderness Outfitters is owned by locals Gary and Kitty Shelton and Earl and Candy Robertson. They operate exclusively on the Middle Fork of the Salmon River, one of the premier whitewater rivers in the United States. Gourmet food highlighted with Dutch oven cooking contributes to many guests rating their six-day float as "the best vacation they've ever had." The Middle Fork is a true Idaho celebrity.

This is my wife Kim's recipe for bread.
She makes it every week.
I'm a lucky man.

Steve Miller

THE STANDARD LOAF
■■■■■■■■■■■■■■■■■■■■■■

Combine in a
large stainless bowl:

6 cups flour
3 tsp. salt
2 tbsp. dry yeast

Combine in a
medium stainless bowl:

2 2/3 cup warm water, about 100°
1 tbsp. butter
1 tbsp. honey or sugar

■■■■■■■■■■■■■■■■■■■■■■■■■■■■■■■■■■■■■■■

Add dry ingredients to wet ingredients. Mix, then turn out onto a floured counter and knead 5 minutes or until smooth. Add more flour as needed to keep it from sticking.

Bread dough should fit into your schedule. At this point you can put dough back into the bowl, covered with a towel. Let rise an hour or so. Then shape into braids, loaves or rolls (stuffed with olives, feta cheese or our favorite, onions).

Let rise another 1/2 hour, or whatever your schedule allows. Bake at 350° for 40-60 minutes until done. Should sound hollow when done.

Dough can also be used for later. Put into a large zip lock bag and put in the refrigerator. It will continue to rise, as you will see.

To use later, remove from fridge, let dough warm up. If sticky, use a little flour. Put into pans, use for pizza, shape into rolls. Let rise and bake.

Clean up: Use wet paper towels for cleaning sticky flour bowls. Let bowl soak full of water a few minutes, then wipe out. Use wet paper towels to clean counter, too.

Steve Miller

Steve Miller formed his first band at the age of 12, and has been making chart-busting music with feverish guitar riffs ever since. Steve changed the economics of rock and roll music by holding out for what was in 1967 a record advance payment for a debut album, and a sizable royalty rate. Those were opportune negotiations, since over the decades hits like *Fly Like an Eagle, Rock 'n Me* and *Take the Money and Run* have hogged the top of the charts for weeks at a time. Steve's latest album, *Wide River*, was recorded at his north county studio.

WARREN MILLER

352 B Beaver Dam Circle
Vail, Colorado 81657
303/476-8967
Fax: 303/476-3846

320 Paani Pl. 4-C
Paia, Hawaii 96779
808/871-5662
Fax: 808/877-2108

WARREN'S FAVORITE SALAD

Frozen peas
Canned mandarin oranges
Slivered almonds
Equal parts, sour cream and mayonnaise
Chopped green onions
Small amount, grated fresh ginger

Mix together portions according to individual taste buds.

Ready when peas thaw.

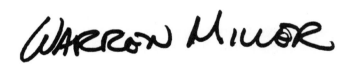

Warren Miller

Locals know that it's time to tune their skis when Warren Miller's latest ski film premieres at the Sun Valley Opera House in late fall. In 1947, Warren spent his first Sun Valley winter living in a van at the River Run parking lot, spending a mere $18. Since then, movies like *Snow Wonder, Born to Ski* and *Extreme Skiing* have made Warren Miller a big name in the sport filming industry. Warren met wife Laurie at the top of Baldy.

INTERNATIONAL SKI VACATION

Post Office Box 5241 • Ketchum, Idaho 83340 • 208-726-3607

DAN MOONEY'S WORLD FAMOUS B.B.Q. CHICKEN

Back in the 70's when myself and a bunch of the guys were ski racing, we didn't have a lot of dough, therefore we had to resort to eating chicken the cheapo way. Often we would improvise on the B.B.Q. sauce to using whatever we had in the refrigerator door. Through this process of trial and error I developed a sauce, that over the years, has gotten rave reviews from my family and friends.

THE SAUCE

1/2 cup of any b.b.q. sauce
1/4 cup ketchup
1/4 cup salsa (the hotter the better)
Tabasco 5-7 shakes
Soy sauce 10-15 shakes
Worschester sauce 10-15 shakes

Mix all ingredients in a large bowl, then add chicken.
VERY IMPORTANT: sauce and chicken must be mixed together with both hands! NO UTENSILS!

The secret to great b.b.q. chicken is to turn and move your meat every 2 to 3 minutes and whatever you do, never let the flame touch the meat. If your fire gets too hot, douse the flame with water and continue cooking. Cooking time: 45 minutes to and hour or so.

ENJOY!

DAN MOONEY

Dan Mooney

Dan Mooney was the first American to beat Jean Claude Killy on the 1972 World Pro Skiing Tour. He was also on the U.S. Ski Team from 1969 to 1972. Dan and his wife recently started International Ski Vacation, offering personally guided ski tours to Europe and South America.

Demi Moore   Bruce Willis

CHOPPED SALAD

Salad

2 heads of romaine lettuce
1/2 head broccoli
1/2 head cauliflower
4 tomatoes
4 stalks of celery
1 16 oz. can of garbanzo beans
4 grilled chicken breasts (optional)

Chop all ingredients very fine.

Dressing

1 cup olive oil
10 tbsp. lemon juice
2 tsp. dijon mustard
2 oz. can of anchovies
1/2 tsp. black pepper
Parmesan cheese to taste

Mix all ingredients in blender.

Variation: Use shrimp or turkey in place of chicken.

Demi Moore

Bruce Willis

Demi Moore and Bruce Willis

The quintessential '90s movie star couple, Demi Moore and Bruce Willis have collaborated on the construction of their Sun Valley home, three children and the movie, *Mortal Thoughts*. Bruce became famous with a five-year run on the popular television comedy series, *Moonlighting*. He then went on to star in memorable feature films such as *Die Hard, Blind Date, In Country* and *Billy Bathgate*, among others. Demi, nominated for a Golden Globe award for Paramount's high-grossing *Ghost*, has also had an exceptional acting career. Pregnancy appeared alluring when she posed for the cover of *Vanity Fair*. In a later *Vanity* cover, Demi answered the question, "Is there life after motherhood?" Demi has since starred in the acclaimed *Indecent Proposal* and *A Few Good Men*. Other leading roles include *St. Elmo's Fire, Blame It On Rio* and *About Last Night*.

Hailey Rodeo Ropers

During the 1930s my grandfather had Arden, one of the great field trial Labrador kennels, named after the family home in New York. Grandfather was a great shot and encouraged all of us to learn to shoot and handle field dogs as children. He was always delighted that whenever we visited him in Washington or Florida, or later in Virginia, we would bring him pheasants.

HARRIMAN HASH

one broiled pheasant
one can of chicken broth
a small onion or a few shallots
2 tbsp. butter
2 tbsp. flour
some heavy cream
thyme

Sauté onions or shallots in butter.
Add flour to make a roux paste.
Add chicken broth gradually, then add cream and thyme to taste.
Have pheasant cooked and cut up into small diced pieces.
Add to sauce.
Transfer to a double boiler.
Heat. If you wish to reheat, use a double boiler. Do not boil sauce.

David H. Mortimer (signature)

David Mortimer

In 1954, David Mortimer became the third generation in his family to visit Sun Valley. He describes the adventure here. "My vivid memories of that three-day trip from mid-Manhattan were not of an endless, arduous journey but of a great adventure involving an overnight train to Chicago and then another all the way to Shoshone where a wood-paneled stationwagon, sent by the Lodge, waited for us at a siding. I'm sure that my mother remembers this expedition less fondly since my cousin and I, both six years old, were her only travelling companions. All of this was to ski on Half Dollar Mountain, but to us it was Himalayan compared to the slanted meadows with rope tows that we were used to in the East." David had arrived at the resort his grandfather Averell Harriman developed for the Union Pacific Railroad. David continues to visit, staying at the Harriman Cottage next to the Sun Valley Lodge.

Mike Murphy

P.O. BOX 4732 • KETCHUM, IDAHO 83340 • 208-622-8845

PAD THAI

THIS IS MY FAVORITE THAI DISH. WE ALWAYS ADD EXTRA
CHILI FLAKES AND SAMBAL PASTE AT THE END FOR THOSE
WHO LOVE IT HOTTTTTT!

12 OUNCES PAD THAI NOODLES OR SOBA NOODLES
8 CUPS COLD WATER

1/4 CUP OLIVE OIL
1 TAB CHOPPED GARLIC
16 MEDIUM SHRIMP, SHELLED AND DEVEINED
2 CHICKEN BREASTS, BROWNED AND CUT INTO SMALL PIECES
2 EGGS BEATEN
1/2 CUP TAMARIND JUICE
1/4 CUP CRUSHED UNSALTED PEANUTS
3 TAB FISH SAUCE
2 1/2 TAB RICE VINEGAR
1 TAB SUGAR OR 1 1/2 TAB HONEY
2 TEA PAPRIKA
1/2 TEA CRUSHED RED PEPPER
3 OUNCES BEAN SPROUTS
1/4 CUP LEEKS CUT INTO 1/12 TO 2 INCH LONG SHREDS

IN A LARGE BOWL, SOAK NOODLES IN COLD WATER 45 MINUTES. DRAIN IN A COLANDER
AND PUT ASIDE.

HEAT OLIVE OIL IN A LARGE SKILLET OVER HIGH HEAT. ADD GARLIC AND SAUTE UNTIL
LIGHTLY BROWNED, ABOUT 1 MINUTE. ADD SHRIMP AND SAUTE 1 MINUTE. ADD
BROWNED CHICKEN, EGGS AND STIR 30 SECONDS. ADD RESERVED NOODLES, TAMARIND
JUICE, PEANUTS, FISH SAUCE, VINEGAR, SUGAR, PAPRIKA, AND RED PEPPER AND STIR
CONSTANTLY 3 MINUTES. REMOVE FROM HEAT AND TRANSFER TO PLATTER. SPRINKLE
WITH BEAN SPROUT AND LEEKS AND SERVE.

ENJOY!!!!!

Mike Murphy

Mike Murphy

Mike Murphy, the "Marathon Man of Comedy," has nimbly coaxed "happy hour laughs"
from weary skiers at Sun Valley's Ram Bar for 16 years. When Mike isn't at the Ram,
you may find him opening for Jerry Seinfeld, Yakov Smirov or Jeff Altman.

Box 474 • Clayton, Idaho 83227 • (208) 879-4677

This recipe is for our favorite mountain pancakes. They are extremely light and I usually serve them with a few good sized pebbles on top to keep them from floating away. Add a little butter and your favorite syrup and enjoy. Because they are so thin, the kids like to pile 'em high.

Joann

MOUNTAIN PANCAKES

1 1/2-2 cups flour
2 tbsp. baking powder

6 eggs
1 tbsp. oil
1/2 cube melted butter
1 1/2 cup milk

Blend the last four items to the flour mixture.
Beat with wire whip and cook on hot griddle.

Make sure to keep the mixture loose and not real thick.

Muzzie Braun & The Boys & Joann

Muzzie Braun and the Boys

The music of Muzzie Braun and the Boys has been heard from the shores of
Redfish Lake to the stage of the Grand Ole Opry to the set of The Tonight Show.
Dad Muzzie and his four sons received the 1989 Wrangler Award for "Best Western Music."
When not performing, the Braun family lives in Clayton, Idaho.

Leif Odmark

If you are going to live it up,
I think you will love this shrimp salad.

SHRIMP SALAD ALA "KETCHUM NORTH"

20 large shrimp, cooked, drained and peeled

With tails intact, cooled, mix with:

3/4 cup heavy cream
2 tbsp. Dijon mustard
1 tbsp. catsup
1 tbsp. minced fresh chives
1 1/2 tsp. Worcestershire sauce
juice of 1/2 lemon
salt and fresh ground pepper
a pinch of tarragon and thyme

Chill and serve with iced Aquavit and a beer chaser,
or a Pouilly Fousse.

Leif Odmark

A resident of Sun Valley since the 1940s, Leif Odmark was a U.S. Olympic nordic coach and a Goodwill Ambassador to the 1972 Sapporo Olympic Games in Japan. Leif founded the Sun Valley Nordic Ski School and Touring Center in 1970, the first of its kind in this country. Leif remains active in the sports world and holds a course record in the St. George Marathon in the 60-years-and-over age category.

SWAMI YOGI MODO'S CHOCOLATE PIE

Pie Crust:

1 cup & 1 tbsp. flour
1/2 tsp. salt
1/3 cup oil
2 tbsp. cold water

Blend flour and salt. Stir in 1/3 cup of oil (maybe more) and 2 tbsp. <u>cold</u> water. Blend into ball and flatten in between two pieces of waxed paper. Set into pie pan and crimp to sides (otherwise, the edges will shrink away during baking). Prick bottom and sides. Bake 425° for 7 to 11 minutes (must watch).

Filling:

2 squares unsweetened chocolate
1 can Eagle Brand sweetened condensed milk
1/4 cup water
vanilla
whipping cream

Using a double boiler, bring water to boil, then lower to low/medium. Add chocolate and milk. Stir over hot water until it thickens (drop from spoon until it is mounding).

Add 1/4 cup water and stir until it is mounding again. Remove from heat and allow to cool. Add 1 tsp. vanilla after chocolate is room temperature. Scoop into pie shell. Whip cream, adding a touch of vanilla and a little powdered sugar. Serve chilled (on top of pie, silly).

This is a rich creamy, chocolate dessert that does not taste like heavy fudge (which I also adore), but is much, much lighter. As a child, I remember that it was just the right amount of sweet to curl my toes, and it's cool, creamy texture always half-closed my eyes and made me smile like a Cheshire cat. Nowadays, as people hide their grocery carts from a real live guru like me, I especially enjoy this fat cat act. You will too. Try it and enter Nirvana!

Richard Michael Odom

Richard Michael Odom

Richard Odom's incredibly soothing yet deliberate voice has guided star and stumbler alike through the most contorting yoga moves for nearly 20 years in the Wood River Valley. The yoga guru quips that his is one of only two professions that people pay to have others sit on them. Attend one of Richard's yoga sessions, and you'll understand his particular brand of humor.

the ORE HOUSE

Sun Valley

I know that the Ore House is famous for its steaks, but our seafood entrees are quickly catching up in popularity. My favorite is the Crab Stuffed Orange Roughy ... I hope it will be yours too!

Lem Sentz

CRAB STUFFED ORANGE ROUGHY (Serves 8)

Ingredients:
8 8-oz. portion filets orange roughy

Mix together:
1 lb. dungeness crabmeat
3 tsp. finely chopped onion
2 tsp. finely chopped red pepper
2 tsp. chopped parsley (fresh or dry)
1 tsp. Pickapeppa
2 tsp. mayonnaise
1 1/2 tsp. ground mustard
2 tsp. "Old Bay" seasoning
1 egg
2/3 cup dry bread crumbs

Divide crabmeat mixture into 8 portions. Place each portion in center of filet and roll up. Place in baking pan. Dot with butter, sprinkle with fresh lemon juice and paprika.

Bake at 350° for 20 minutes.

Lem Sentz

P.O. Box 282   Sun Valley, Idaho 83353   (208) 622-4363

The Ore House

Since 1966, the Ore House has attracted tourists and locals to their boardwalk mall location. Surrounded by aspen, the large wooden deck is a perfect place to indulge in one of their famous Idaho steaks and to watch people walking by. During the winter, skiers apres-ski in an Old West decor with Bama prints and stuffed birds and game.

ARLENE'S ZUCCHINI BAKE

2 large zucchini, sliced lengthwise
2 large tomatoes, sliced
1 large onion, sliced
1 cup mushrooms, sliced
1/2 cup parmesan cheese, grated or shredded

Layer in the above order 2 times in a non-greased baking dish. Bake uncovered for 30 minutes at 350□.

This dish is delicious, nutritious, low in fat, and quick and easy to make. Great as a main course with rice!

Thanks, Mom!

Gretchen Palmer

Gretchen Palmer

Gretchen Palmer has been involved in all aspects of the sports modeling and photography world. Gretchen can be recognized in advertisements for *Eddie Bauer, Bogner, Skiing* magazine, *Ski Magazine* and *LL Bean*. Gretchen now runs her own modeling and production company in Sun Valley.

97

PALMER'S PECAN POPOVERS

Dough:

2 eggs
1 cup milk
1/2 tsp. salt
1 cup flour
1/4 cup finely chopped pecans

Lemon-honey butter:

6 tbsp. softened butter
6 tbsp. honey
3/4 tsp. finely mined zest of lemon

Preheat oven to 425°. Grease 6, 5-6 oz. custard cups.

To prepare popovers: With a wire whisk, beat together eggs, milk, and salt. Add flour and beat just until smooth, being careful not to overbeat. Stir in pecans and pour into custard cups. Bake until puffed and golden brown - 30 to 35 minutes. Remove from cups and serve immediately.

To prepare lemon-honey butter: Stir together butter, honey, and zest and spread on warm popovers.

Yield 6 popovers

Terry Palmer

Terry Palmer was a member of the 1972 U.S. Olympic alpine team.
The same year he was the U.S. National Slalom champion. During his pro-skiing years,
Terry took first place in the 1976 Lange Cup and was a Number One Pacesetter for Nastar in 1978.
Terry continues on the cutting edge as a ski-design consultant.

OATMEAL COOKIES

3 eggs
1 cup raisins
1 cup sugar
1 tsp. vanilla
1 1/2 cup flour
1 tsp. salt
1 tsp. soda
3 cups old fashioned oats
1 cup chocolate chips (optional)
1 cup shortening

Mixing procedure:

Whip eggs and vanilla together, add raisins.
Let stand for one hour. Cream shortening and sugar.
Add eggs, vanilla, raisins, salt, soda. Mix well.

Add flour, oats, and chocolate chips (if desired).
Form small balls of cookie dough, flatten with a fork, and
place on a greased cookie sheet. Or, flatten the dough until it
covers the bottom of the cookie sheet.
Bake at 350. Cut into squares when done.

Christello Parrish

Christello Parrish

BOX 301 SUN VALLEY, IDAHO 83353

Lane Parrish
This recipe was contributed in memory of Lane Parrish by his family.
The Hollywood stunt man was known nationwide for daring aerial ski tricks and in
Ketchum by a throng of friends for cooking outrageous dinners and bow hunting.
A hiking trail at nearby Adam's Gulch was lovingly built for and named after Lane.

RIDLEY PEARSON
P.O. Box 670 - Hailey, Idaho 93333

UMBRIAN SPIT-ROASTED CHICKEN - IDAHO MEETS ITALY

NOTE: There is no need to spit on the chicken in order to make this delicious central-Italy dish. Instead, trot on down to your hardware store and buy a motor-driven rotisserie, or, for the more aerobically inclined, shove a piece of rebar through the bird, affix a wooden handle and sit there for an hour spinning the old bird above the glowing embers.

1, 3 or 4 lb. chicken: satisfies 4 hungry, 6 light, appetites

NEED:
1 whole roasting chicken; (remove and discard giblets - who likes those things, anyway?). Wash thoroughly with cold water, pat dry with towel - don't forget the cavity!

3 cloves garlic, 1/4 cup olive oil, 4 sprigs fresh rosemary, salt and pepper.

Chop garlic into hefty chunks. Along with 1 sprig of rosemary, place garlic into the bird cavity. Tie legs and arms - chicken bondage - with baking string. Slather bird with olive oil, all over. Strip remaining rosemary from stems and chop it coarsely - what a smell! Pat rosemary onto chicken body - chicken massage; liberally salt and pepper; skewer onto rotisserie rod or rebar; cook fairly low over charcoal or wood fire (I prefer charcoal and mesquite chunks that have been soaked in water for one hour - soak the mesquite, not the charcoal!) for approximately 20 minutes a lb., about an hour and a quarter; meat thermometer temp. at thigh should be about 370.

NOTE: Those who can't find rebar or are too cheap to buy a motorized rotisserie: If oven cooking, preheat to 375, cook approximately 20 minutes per lb. to same body temperature as above. This is good, but there's something special - and *very* Italian - about the moto-roto.

Serve (separate courses) with pasta and sautéed chunks of eggplant (course one), chicken (two) and orange sherbet (three).

Stag's Leap (or other) Merlot, or a very fine Chianti Classico, highly recommended - but not for those who might be driving the chicken rebar. Warning: Alcohol impairs motor coordination - but not electric motors!

Ridley Pearson

Ridley Pearson is the author of seven novels, including best sellers *Undercurrents* and *Probable Cause*. His work has been translated into fourteen languages. Ridley was the first American awarded the Raymond Chandler/Fulbright Fellowship in detective fiction. The author plays electric bass guitar in the literary supergroup, The Rock-Bottom Remainders, and the local megagroup, The Sensational Toast Points. Ridley and his wife, writer/editor Colleen Daly, live in south county.

FLAT TOP SHEEP CO.

JOHN T. PEAVEY, PRES.

P.O. Box 88
Carey, Idaho 83320

Summer (208) 788-2850
Winter (208) 726-7568

FLAT TOP SHEEP COMPANY LAMB SHANKS

FLAT TOP SHEEP COMPANY has been in the Peavey family for three generations, now moving into its fourth. When people visit the ranch they most remember the vast space. It is a working ranch surrounded by miles of tall grasses, rolling sagebrush hills and basalt rock ridges.

Our house is a series of cabins strung together into an L, brought here by Jim Laidlaw, the original ranch owner, in the 1880's from the nearby Muldoon mines. Throughout the spring, summer and fall, the house is teeming with activity. Picnics and lamb or beef barbecues are regular events. Usually after tapenade dip with fresh summer vegetables and a plate of smoked fish or cheeses - and just before the lamb goes on the grill - we take our guests up to the knoll across from the ranch house. There on the peak is the spectacular site of Jim Laidlaw's grave. The wake for Laidlaw is legendary and there is still part of a case of Johnny Walker Black Label Scotch buried with the old man.

Several years ago, we began putting our favorite lamb and beef recipes on cards to hand out during John's state senate campaigns. This recipe was originally suggested by my mother, Mary Brooks, was then jazzed up a bit by Diane. A real family effort. It is a favorite, maybe because it's so easy.

Flat Top Sheep Company Lamb Shanks

4 lamb shanks
1 package dry onion soup mix
Rosemary (fresh, if available)
Fresh garlic slivers

Place each lamb shank on a separate piece of aluminum foil large enough to wrap around the meat. Sprinkle 1/4 of the onion soup mix over each shank. Liberally, cut slits on top and bottom of the lamb and put pieces of slivered garlic in each slit. Sprinkle with rosemary, and fresh ground pepper. Wrap each shank in its sheet of foil and put the four packets in a slow oven at 275 degrees just after lunch. By dinner, the lamb will be falling-off-the-bone-tender and ready to eat.

John Peavey
Diane Joseph Peavey

Diane and John Peavey

John and Diane Peavey live and work the family's four-generations-old sheep and cattle ranch north of Carey with son Tom and mother Mary Brooks. John is the state senator for Blaine County and Diane is a writer and fanatic cook, particularly at the ranch, located 24 dirt-road miles from town.

MARINATED ELK OR VENISON FILET

2 - 3 c. red wine
¼ c. red wine vinegar
1 sliced onion
1 grated carrot
¼ c. fresh chopped parsley

1 T. dried thyme
2 - 3 sliced garlic cloves
1 t. peppercorns
3 - 4 junniper berries
3 T. olive oil

Cut elk or venison steak into 4 - 6 individual portions and marinate in the above sauce for approximately 24 hours. Remove steaks and let them dry at room temperature for about 15 minutes before cooking. The steaks may be barbequed or sautéd in a frying pan or cast iron skillet. Game meat is tastiest when cooked on a hot fire and served rare!

For special occasions it is worth the extra time spent to use the marinade to make a sauce for the meat. Strain the marinade into a pan and boil. Reduce to about 2 T. Add and heat (do not boil) the following ingredients:

1 - 2 c. beef demiglace
1¼ t. dijon mustard
1 - 2 T. red currant jelly

3 - 4 T. port wine
2 T. butter (optional)

ENJOY !!

Kristy Pigeon

Kristy Pigeon

Kristy Pigeon won the Wimbledon Junior Tennis Championship in 1968 and, later, was ranked among the world's top ten women players. Kristy developed the Sagebrush Arena, an equestrian facility, located just north of Hailey. She now directs a therapeutic riding program for individuals with physical and mental disabilities.

2 6-oz. jars marinated
    artichoke hearts
1 small onion,
    finely chopped
1 garlic clove, minced
4 eggs
1/4 cup fine bread or
    cracker crumbs
1/4 tsp. salt
2 tbsp. minced parsley
1/8 tsp. pepper
1/8 tsp. oregano
1/8 tsp. Tabasco sauce
2 cups grated sharp cheddar cheese

ARTICHOKE FRITTATA

Drain marinade from 1 jar of artichokes into medium skillet. Drain second jar and discard marinade. Add onion and garlic to skillet and sauté until onion is limp. Chop all artichokes and set aside.

In a bowl, beat eggs with a fork and add remaining ingredients. Stir in onion mixture and artichokes. Pour into a greased 7x11 inch baking dish. Bake uncovered at 325° for 30 minutes.

Cool and cut into 1-inch squares. Use toothpicks if desired.

Note: Freezes beautifully.

I add mushrooms, bell pepper, tomato or zucchini. Can be served in a pie pan like a quiche.

I serve it as an hors d'oeuvre. Great to serve with salad and roll for a vegetarian dinner.

Enjoy!

HANSING HOUSE • HAILEY, IDAHO

Pat Priest

Pat Priest Hansing played the "normal one" on the television show *The Munsters*. She was the perky, blond and bouffant-coiffed niece, Marilyn. Pat says her life has moved in a complete circle: She was raised in the small Utah town of Bountiful, ran the rat race in Washington, D.C., and Hollywood, and she says "now I'm back living in a small town, Hailey, Idaho, and I love it."

SPOTTED DICK DESSERT

6 LARGE RIPE BANANAS
6 WOODEN POPSICLE STICKS
4 LARGE CHOCOLATE BARS
1/4 CUP WHITE CHOCOLATE

INSERT POPSICLE STICKS INTO PEELED BANANAS. PLACE IN FREEZER OVERNIGHT. MELT CHOCOLATE ON LOW HEAT IN DOUBLE BOILER. GRATE WHITE CHOCOLATE INTO SHALLOW PLATE OR PIE TIN.

WHEN CHOCOLATE IS MELTED, REMOVE BANANAS FROM FREEZER AND IMMEDIATELY DIP INTO WARM CHOCOLATE, MAKING SURE TO COMPLETELY COVER THE SURFACE OF BANANA. ROLL INTO WHITE CHOCOLATE. ENJOY WITH PLENTY OF NAPKINS.

VARIATION: ROLL BANANAS IN FINELY CHOPPED CASHEWS.

Brian W. Sturges

Debbie Edgers Sturges

The Sturges Society
Debbie Edgers/Brian Sturges Est. 9/4/89
The Red Dog Gallery and Bluebird Supply
Box 1556 Ketchum, ID 83340 (208) 726-2602

Red Dog Gallery and Bluebird Supply

Forging a path through art frontiers, Debbie Edgers' bright paintings, often featuring spotted dogs, can best be described as "contemporary folk art." Her art is owned by the McDonald's Corporation and Alaska First Federal Credit Union collections. Debbie's husband, Brian Sturges, is Ketchum's top birdwatcher and advocate for feathered friends. Together, they own the Red Dog Gallery and Bluebird Supply, a gallery blending art and nature.

REDFISH LAKE LODGE

5 MILES SOUTH OF STANLEY, IDAHO
— *IN THE HEART OF THE SAWTOOTH MOUNTAINS* —
PHONE - AREA CODE 208 - STANLEY 774-3536

JACK SEE, Manager

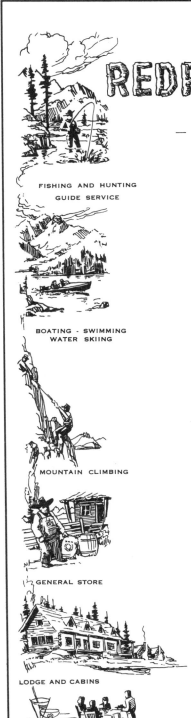

FISHING AND HUNTING GUIDE SERVICE

BOATING - SWIMMING WATER SKIING

MOUNTAIN CLIMBING

GENERAL STORE

LODGE AND CABINS

BAR AND DINING ROOM

HORSEBACK RIDING PACK TRIPS

HIKING - SIGHTSEEING

SERVICE STATION

PAVED ACCESS ROADS FROM U.S. 93 - U.S. 30

TRAILER PARKING AND PICNIC AREA

FAMILY FUN AND RECREATION

FAMOUS POTATOES - BASQUE SOUP

This soup is a combination of two of the many things that make Idaho the great place it is.

Ingredients:

3 lbs. Basque chorizo links
1 doz. peeled and diced Idaho spuds
1 doz. peeled, seeded and diced tomatoes
6 cups peeled, seeded and diced Anaheim chiles
2 cups diced small yellow onions
1 cup chopped fine garlic
2 tbsp. each fresh ground black pepper and oregano
2 gallons chicken stock

Slice chorizo into thin rounds and cook them in a medium size heavy-bottom stock pot. Add garlic, onions, and chiles and cook until the chiles are soft and the onions clear. Add chicken stock, pepper and oregano and bring to a boil. Add potatoes and simmer until potatoes are done, but firm. Add tomatoes and serve!

Serves an army!

Mike

REDFISH LAKE LODGE
Stanley, Idaho 83278

Redfish Lake Lodge

Redfish Lake Lodge, located in the heart of the Sawtooth Mountain Range, is owned and operated by the Jack See family. Guests staying at the timeless log lodge, built in 1928, enjoy Western-style hospitality in tranquil surroundings. Sitting on the veranda and watching the sun slide into the craggy granite peaks is one of life's basic pleasures.

BEEF TENDERLOIN

Whole beef tenderloin, cleaned and peeled

Cover with olive oil.

Coat with: rosemary, crushed
             garlic, lots
             kosher salt, some
             coarse ground black pepper

Bake in oven at 225°for 1 1/2 hours.
Finish on charcoal grill 1/2 hour to 1 hour,
add more kosher salt.

Tim Kohl

Research Dynamics

From peon to president, the six employees at Research Dynamics all answer phones, make
coffee and design and test the company's latest skis and mountain bikes. During the winter, you may
see President Tim Kohl shredding the bumps on Exhibition. Likewise, a peon might have the pleasure
of taking an RD mountain bike to the extreme. Peon or president, someone has gotta do it!

SHARI RHOADS
BRUCHMATTHALDE 3
CH - 6003 LUCERNE
SWITZERLAND

Here is a favorite recipe of mine for a moist, spicy cake that never fails.
It's an old WWII recipe; eggs and butter were scarce then.

POOR MAN'S CAKE

Simmer for 5 minutes:

2 cubes of margarine (or butter)
2 1/4 cups water
1 1/2 cups sugar
1 cup raisins

Cool to room temperature and then add:

3 cups flour
1 1/2 tsp. soda
1 1/2 tsp. salt
1 1/2 tsp. baking powder
1 1/2 tsp. cinnamon
1 1/2 tsp. nutmeg
1 cup chopped walnuts

Pour into a buttered and floured 9x13 inch cake pan and
bake at 350° for 25-30 minutes. Cool and frost with
cream cheese frosting.

Shari Rhoads

Fifth-generation Idahoan Shari Rhoads has accompanied in concert many of the great opera singers of our time, including Montserrat Caballè, Josè Carreras and Placido Domingo. When Shari began conducting opera five years ago in Europe, audiences usually assumed she was a harpist or flutist. In the first upbeat of the overture, Shari says, "One could hear an audible gasp that a girl was wielding the holy baton." Shari's husband, Jeffrey Agrell, is writing an eco-suspense novel based in this area.

River Grove Ravioli

2 pkgs. fresh ravioli (chicken or cheese)
1 container pesto sauce
1 rotisserie chicken
1 jar sun dried tomatoes (in oil)
pine nuts
Parmesan cheese

Cook pasta, toss with pesto sauce, add cut up chicken and chopped sundried tomatoes. Add as many pine nuts as you would like. Pass cheese at table. Serve with hot crusty bread.

Box 2029   Hailey, ID 83333

River Grove Farm

Recognizable by its white fences and immaculate grounds, River Grove Farm, north of Hailey, is home to some of the nation's top hunting, jumping and dressage horses. Trainers Debbie and Bob McDonald and owners E. Parry and Peggy Thomas travel every April and October to Europe where they purchase top young horses. Debbie rode River Grove's Whisper to the first-level American Horse Show Association Championship in 1992.

Mary Rolland

BUTTERSCOTCH BROWNIES

2 cups light brown sugar
(finger sift to remove any lumps)
1 1/2 sticks margarine or butter (melted)
2 cups flour (finger sift)
2 tsp. baking powder
1 tsp. salt
2 tsp. vanilla
2 eggs (lightly beaten)
1 1/2 cups chopped nuts

Stir melted butter into brown sugar and set aside.
Mix flour, salt and baking powder together and add to brown sugar mixture.

Add vanilla to eggs and beat lightly. Mix into flour mixture. Stir in nuts.

Bake in a greased and floured 9x11 dish and put into a preheated oven at 350°. Bake about 40 minutes, or until brownies test done with a toothpick or knife.

If the brownies are too dry, next time add more butter.
If they are too gooey, add less butter and cook longer.
Don't get discouraged! Once you get the perfect batch,
you'll have friends for life!

Mary Rolland

476 Broadway   NYC, NY 10013   212-925-9440

Mary Rolland

Mary Rolland lived in Sun Valley during the 1970s and now draws on its "special magic and spirit" to enhance her art. She counts herself a survivor, having lived in New York City for thirteen years. Mary's art is in hundreds of private collections throughout the United States.

HALIBUT
ROSE CREEK

3-4 servings

1 to 1 1/2 pounds halibut steak
salt
lemon juice
2 small tomatoes, chopped
1 medium onion, finely minced
2 cloves garlic, crushed
1/4 c. olive oil
pinch of sugar

1/4 c. chopped fresh
    parsley
3 tbsp. tomato paste
3/4 c. Rose Creek Idaho
    chardonnay
1/2 c. water
3 slices of lemon
1 sliced tomato

Place halibut in an oiled shallow baking dish. Sprinkle with salt and a few drops of lemon juice. In a separate pan, simmer tomatoes, onion and garlic in olive oil until soft and golden. Add a pinch of sugar, the parsley, tomato paste and chardonnay. Simmer until well blended. Add water, stirring to blend.

Pour sauce over fish; top with lemon and tomato slices. Cover dish completely with aluminum foil, wrapping foil around bottom of dish.
Bake at 375 for 20 - 30 minutes.
Serve with fluffy rice.

My choice of wine to accompany this dish is an Idaho Chardonnay.

Elaine

Jamie Martin
Winemaker

River Views

Pamela Swanson Kerr

Rose Creek

Rose Creek Winery

The Snake River Canyon offers volcanic soils, long sunny days and spring water from the
Lost River Aquifer. These create the optimum elements for growing fine wine grapes.
The Rose Creek winery, owned by winemaker Jamie Martin and family, is constructed of native lava.
Its three-foot thick walls maintain the proper temperatures for wine making and cooperage.

P.O. Box 900
Beverly Hills, California 90213
Phone 310 203 4526 • Fax 310 203 4690

FOX NEWS
A UNIT OF FOX INC.

Van Gordon Sauter
President

Anything I generate in a kitchen is either outrageously unhealthy or politically incorrect. So let me draw upon the skill of my sainted mother-in-law, Bernice Brown, the former First Lady of California. Years ago, as the wife of Gov. Edmund G. Brown, she prepared banana cakes for countless raffles and fund raising auctions. The banana cake derived from her recipe is astonishingly good and to this day is highly regarded among Sacramento afficionados. One night a cake of Bernice's was up for bid during an unusually slow fundraising program on the local PBS station. To accelerate the bidding, one of Bernice's daughters (not my wife) surreptitiously bid $25, a hardly inconsequential offering in the early 60s. The Governor, a keen admirer of his wife's culinary skills, phoned the station and exuberantly doubled that bid. Bernice's appreciation of this grandiose gesture was quickly deflated when the Governor ... suddenly realizing he just paid $50 for a cake no different from one downstairs in the Governor's Mansion refrigerator ... blurted out that, well, the cake is marvelous, but probably not worth that kind of money. Bernice soon made it clear to him that works of art should not be subjected to crass financial analysis. And believe me, what derives from this recipe is a legitimate work art.

BANANA CAKE

1/2 Cup butter
1 1/2 Cups sugar
2 Eggs
1/2 Cup sour milk or
1/4 Cup buttermilk

1 Tsp baking soda
2 Cups flour
2 Tsp Calumet baking powder
3 Bananas, mashed
1 Tsp vanilla
1 Cup walnuts, chopped

Cream butter and sugar. Add egg yolks, then milk with baking soda. Mix. Add flour and baking powder sifted together. Add vanilla, bananas and nuts and beat well. Fold in beaten egg whites. Bake in 3 greased layer pans in a 325 to 350 oven until done (about 1/2 hour).

Spread with the following icing:

2 Tbsp - Butter
2 1/2 Cups confectioner's sugar

1 Whole egg
1 Tsp Cream or top milk

Cream butter and sugar. Add whole egg. Add vanilla. Add cream until the icing is the right consistency to spread.

Van Gordon Sauter

Van Gordon Sauter, president of Fox News, and his wife Kathleen Brown,
treasurer of the State of California, find time to get away to their Sun Valley
home between international crises and the latest fiscal crunch.

CHICKEN SENEGALESE

This dish was inspired by a curry, chicken and apple soup I enjoyed in the country of Senegal, West Africa. It is now one of the most popular entrees at our restaurant.

Ingredients (for 2 servings)

4 boneless, skinless chicken breasts
white flour
shallots
dry sherry
apple juice
hot curry powder
medium curry powder
heavy whipping cream
salt/pepper
thinly sliced green apple

Heat 1 1/2 ounces of drawn butter in a 10-oz. sauté pan. Lightly coat the chicken breasts in the flour and brown the breasts in the butter on both sides, approximately 2 minutes per side. Add a healthy pinch of shallots and cook until they are just turning translucent, approximately 30 seconds or so.

Add about 4 oz. of dry sherry and 4 oz. of high-quality apple juice. Add 1 tsp. of hot curry powder and 1 tsp. of medium curry powder. Reduce all of this until it is thickened and bubbling vigorously.

Add about 5 oz. of old-fashioned heavy whipping cream and swirl the pan briskly, mixing all ingredients thoroughly. Reduce down to the proper thickness and color, a rich, creamy, yellowish brown.

Turn the chicken breasts a couple of times during this period. Add 8 thin slices of green apple about 1 minute before removing the pan from the heat.

Place the chicken on the plates with the apple slices arranged on top, and pour the sauce from the pan over all.

the Sawtooth Club

Natural Mesquite Wood Cooking • Fine Wines • Cocktails

TOM NICKEL

231 N. Main St. • P.O. Box 4316 • Ketchum, ID 83340 • 208-726-5233

The Sawtooth Club

On Friday night, after a sweaty workout at the club or an end-of-ski-day, non-stop run down Old Olympic, many locals head to the Sawtooth Club for a game of backgammon or a cold glass of Sun Valley Ale. The Sawtooth Club has been voted by natives as the "Valley's Best Bar" and the "Valley's Best Restaurant" for the last three years.

Arnold's Eggplant Stack
As created by Michael Rosen
Chef at Schatzi
A Schwarzenegger-Shriver venture

Eggplant (choose size for desired diameter of stack)
Roma tomatoes
imported buffalo mozzarella
extra virgin olive oil
chopped garlic
basil
arrugula
salt
balsamic dressing
coarse black pepper

Cut eggplant into 3/8 - 1/2 inch slices. Brush with olive oil, garlic, salt, pepper and grill or cook under broiler on one side only. Cool slices. Do not cook too much or eggplant will become too soft.

Slice Roma tomatoes about 1/4 inch thick.

Slice buffalo mozzarella 3/8 inch thick (same as eggplant).

Layer eggplant (browned side up) and buffalo mozzarella. The cheese should be slightly inside the edge of the eggplant. Eggplant-cheese, eggplant-cheese, eggplant. Save the nicest slice for the top of the stack. Arrange sliced Roma tomatoes on top, drizzle with olive oil, garlic, salt and black pepper. Cook stack under broiler, not too close to the flame so the tomatoes brown slightly just as the cheese starts to melt. Finish with a chiffonade of basil and serve over arrugula dressed with balsamic dressing.

Schatzi on Main
3110 Main Street
Suite 132
Santa Monica, CA 90405
(310) 399-4800
Fax (310) 399-6868

Arnold Schwarzenegger

In the local weight room, guys exclaim "Can you believe those calves?" On Baldy, ski instructors note, "He really knows how to dice it!" And his movies sell out at the downtown theatre as you would expect from the world's highest-paid movie star. Although Sun Valley is famous for giving its stars elbow-room, some folks just can't resist asking Arnold Schwarzenegger and his wife, Maria Shriver, for an autograph.

SCOTT/MATHAUSER CORP.

BOX 1333 • SUN VALLEY • IDAHO • 83353 • U.S.A • 208-726-5432

GOURMET POACHED HALIBUT OR SALMON FILLETS

Ingredients:

halibut or salmon fillets
1 cup good white wine
basil
dill
tarragon

In a large pot, add enough water to cover the fish you are about to poach. Add approximately 1 cup of a good white wine, along with basil, dill, taragon or your own favorite bouquet garni. Simmer about 20 minutes.

Add the fish fillets and simmer approximately 10 - 15 minutes.

Sauce for fillets:

Use any good commercial tartar sauce (or make your own). Add capers and prepared, pure horseradish, to taste.

Scotty

Ed Scott

Inventor Ed "Scotty" Scott has been beaming up new ideas from this valley since the mid 1940s. His inventions have gone international in a big way from Scott Ski Poles to his latest design, bicycle brake shoes. Some folks call Scotty the "ski pole guru."

114

Ριπσ Γουλαση Σουπ
or
Rips Goulash Zuppa

This hearty goulash soup, has been developed over the years through a combination of trial and error, add or omit, taste and change, and just a pinch of "culinary plagiarism". But....... once you have tasted this dish you'll have more respect for the Hungarians! Try it with freshly baked sourdough bread and garlic/basil olive oil, a fresh green salad, and a good bottle of Zinfandel.

Rip Sewell

Goulash Soup
Six servings

1 pound of pork loin
1 pound beef shanks
1/4 cup lard or vegetable oil
1 large onion chopped
1 1/2 Tbls hot Hungarian paprika
2 teaspoons caraway seeds
1 bay leaf
2 Tbls finely chopped garlic
3 large potatoes, peeled, and cut into 1/2 inch dice.
1/2 green bell pepper, finely chopped
1/2 tomato seeded and diced
4 cups beef stock or canned broth
Salt and freshly ground pepper
Sour cream
Chopped fresh parsley

Remove meat from bones, and cut into 1/4 inch dice. Melt lard in heavy large pot over medium heat and brown about 15 minutes. Add onion paprika, caraway and bay leaf and saute five minutes. Add garlic and saute one minute. Add potatoes, bell pepper, and tomato, stir 1 minute. Add stock and bring to boil. Reduce heat, cover and simmer 30 minutes. Uncover and simmer until beef is tender, adding more stock if thinner consistency is desired, about 1 hour. Add salt and pepper. Ladle into soup bowls and top with sour cream and sprinkle with parsley.

Bon Appetit!!!

Rip Sewell

A job working for Union Pacific Railroad first lured Rip Sewell to Sun Valley in 1953. This husky, father of seven debuted in motion pictures in 1992 when he starred in the locally filmed, nationally released movie *Dark Horse*. Rip is proud that he once coached and "owned the franchise" for The Rippers, a local, world-class ladies' slow pitch team.

3110 Main Street, Suite 132, Santa Monica, CA 90405

Telephone (310) 399-4800 • Fax (310) 399-6868

MARIA'S ORIENTAL CHICKEN SALAD
As created by Michael Rosen, chef at Schatzi,
A Schwarzenegger-Shriver venture

1/4 - 1/2 lb. mixed greens
1 piece (head) Iceberg lettuce
1 bunch watercress tops
1 bunch cilantro
1 bunch mint leaves
1 large carrot
Sesame rice wine vinaigrette

1 small cucumber
3 large oranges
1/2 cup toasted slivered almonds
1 pinch pickled ginger
2 lb. roasted, marinated, boneless chicken
  breasts
Garnish: fried won ton skins

1. Clean lettuce, spin dry and chill for crispness. You can mix watercress, mint and cilantro with lettuces.
2. Peel and julienne the carrot and cucumber. Peel and segment three oranges.
3. Toast almonds.
4. Place all ingredients except won ton skins in a large mixing bowl. Dress lightly with vinaigrette and toss gently. Add more dressing as required. Garnish with won ton skins.

Should make enough for four luncheon salads.

SESAME-RICE WINE VINAIGRETTE

1 cup rice wine vinegar
1/4 cup sugar (to taste)
1 1/2 tsp. black pepper coarse ground
1/2 tsp. crushed red chili pepper

1 tbsp. low sodium soy sauce
1/8 cup dark sesame oil
1/2 cup peanut oil
salt to taste

Wisk all ingredients together.

MARINADE FOR CHICKEN BREAST

1 cup low sodium soy sauce
3 oz. green onions, chopped
1 1/2 oz. ginger, peeled and julienned
2-3 oz. dark sesame oil

Mix together salt and black pepper to taste.
Marinate chicken, overnight is preferable.
Cook skin side up in a 350□ oven for approximately 30 minutes or until done.
Cool and remove skin. Shred chicken breast and set aside.

Maria Shriver

Maria Shriver, TV journalist with her own prime-time show, *First Person with Maria Shriver,* and super mom, calls Sun Valley home whenever she and husband Arnold Schwarzenegger can get away. As a child, Maria remembers visiting Sun Valley with her family and the rest of the Kennedy clan.

CYNTHIA SIKES

BANANA NUT CAKE

An interesting dilemma with this recipe is that it's hard to keep your ripe bananas from being thrown out - you must guard them carefully. I finally had to put a sign on them - "They're brown for a reason!"

<u>Ingredients:</u>
2 eggs

1-1/2 cups sugar
1/2 cup butter
1/2 cup sour milk (1 teaspoon vinegar in milk)

2 cups flour
1 teaspoon baking soda
1 teaspoon baking powder
1/2 teaspoon salt

3 ripe bananas
1 teaspoon vanilla
1/2 cup finely chopped nuts

1)   Separate 2 eggs. In a mixer, beat the egg whites until stiff and then set aside.

2)   In a large bowl, cream together sugar, egg yolks and butter.

3)   Add sour milk and mix thoroughly.

4)   Mix the flour, baking soda, baking powder and salt together and add to the sugar/eggs mixture, blending thoroughly.

5)   Mash 3 ripe bananas with a fork along with a teaspoon of vanilla. Add to the mixture and blend thoroughly. Beat this mixture very well.

6)   Add nuts.

7)   Fold in the egg whites.

Pour mixture into an oblong pan, greased and floured. (Round cake pans may be substituted to make a layer cake.)

Bake at 375 Degrees for 30 - 45 minutes.

ICING FOR BANANA NUT CAKE

In a sauce pan, melt 1/2 stick of butter. Add one Tablespoon of Lemon Juice. Add one ripe, mashed banana and then take from heat.

Add enough Sifted Powdered Sugar to thicken mixture to a glaze. Pour this over the cake while the cake is still hot.

Cynthia Sikes

Cynthia Sikes appeared on several *L.A. Law* episodes as a judge and one of Arnie Becker's love interests and on Broadway as a star in Stephen Sondheim's *Into the Woods.* Cynthia's husband, Bud Yorkin, created, wrote, directed and produced *Maude, The Jeffersons, All In The Family* and produced *Blade Runner.* They have enjoyed the solitude and clean air of Blaine County since the mid '80s.

EVERGREEN RESTAURANT
A BISTRO

ASIAN CURED SALMON (GRAVLAKS SOUTH)

3-4 lbs. very fresh side or sides of salmon, all bones removed, skin on
3 T. sugar
3 T. kosher salt
1 T. roasted and ground Szechwan pepper corns
several twists of black pepper
1 cup coarsely chopped fresh coriander stems and leaves
1/4 cup fresh ginger - 1/16" julienne

Place the salmon sides, skin side down on a rack, on a sheet pan.
Combine all the spices and sprinkle evenly over both sides, all of it. Put the ginger on next, followed by the coriander.
Quickly mate the spiced sides against each other. Wrap over the top with plastic film.
Then put a sheet pan with 16 oz. or so of weight on top of the fish. Refrigerate for 2 days, flipping the fish over in the morning and then in the evening flip it again. Drain any liquid that accumulates.
After 2 days, scrape all the spice away with the back of a knife and slice paper thin for cold use with mustard sauce and pickled onions.
Slice into 1/2" thick filets through the skin for very quick grilling.

OFFICE. 208-726-4406 · FAX 208-726-9365 · P.O. BOX 2560 · SUN VALLEY. IDAHO 83353

Rick Slone

Rick Slone is the author of *Brown Shoe*, published in 1992 by Random House.
When not writing mysteries, Rick is a saute cook at Evergreen Bistro and enjoys life with wife Joyce and son Cary. Rick has been a photographer, elementary school teacher, mountain climber, private detective and carpenter.

118

Andrew Slough

Post Office Box 1359 Sun Valley. Idaho 83353

I must admit I had reservations about releasing this haute cuisine to the general public, but I believe anyone who buys this book will treat this dish with the reverence it deserves. I wish I could say "Ketchup Chicken" has been passed from mother to daughter in my family for five generations, but in truth I invented it while in college. Living on twenty dollars a week left little for anything but basics. Chicken was cheap and hoping to impress a lovely Art History major, I invented my own sauce. In a moment that rivaled Alexander Graham Bell's invention of the telephone, the ingredients miraculously combined in an ode to American cooking. Since then I have only prepared this for close friends and my own boys, who I hope will one day pass this unique and very exciting recipe to their own sons.

KETCHUP CHICKEN ALA ELMER

Ingredients:

2 cut up fryer chickens
2 cups ketchup (brand left to personal taste)
1 cup brown sugar
1/4 cup Lea and Perrins
1 tsp. salt
3 cloves garlic
1 large yellow onion
ground pepper to taste
Bottle of cheap (but not too cheap!) burgundy

Directions:

Combine ketchup, brown sugar, Lea and Perrins, salt, crushed garlic and chopped onion in a bowl and stir well. Add pepper last and set to one side.

Dredge the chicken parts in flour, salt and pepper. Cover bottom of large frying pan (which has a lid) with oil and fry chicken on both sides until light brown.

As soon as chicken is browned, drain off the oil. Using a spoon, cover the skin side of the chicken part (or skinless side, if you strip the skin off) with sauce. Keeping the burner on a medium heat, pour the burgundy into the bottom of the pan and cover. As soon as the burgundy reaches a low boil and begins to reduce, spoon the thickened wine over the chicken. Baste every ten minutes until the chicken is tender. Serve with Tater Tots and salad with Italian dressing.

Please don't share Ketchup Chicken Ala Elmer with your friends,
as I'm thinking of opening a restaurant.

Andrew E. Slough

Andrew Slough

Andy Slough has traveled from the Soviet Union to South America researching articles he has written for *Outside, Sports Illustrated, Conde Nast Traveler* and *Powder* magazines, to name a few. Andy also works as a contributing editor for *Ski Magazine* and has authored a book published by Doubleday titled *The Traveling Skier.* He is presently working on a novel and a children's book.

ANN SOTHERN

SOTHERN DRUMS

2 pkgs. drumsticks
1/2 red pepper
1/2 green pepper
1 large onion, finely chopped
6 fresh mushrooms, cup up
3/4 cup chopped celery
5 carrots, sliced lengthwise, very thin
1 cube chicken bouillon
1 can "Franco American" chicken gravy

1. Sauté chicken with flour, paprika, seasoned salt.

2. Saute vegetables separately with 2 tbsp. oil until tender.

3. Put chicken in electric skillet, cover with the vegetables. Cook at 250□ for 1 1/2 hours.

4. Sprinkle bouillon cube over the mixture.

5. After dish is finished, cover with one can "Franco American" chicken gravy. Let heat.

6. Serve over rice or noodles. Serves 4 easily.

Bon appetit!

Ann Sothern

Ann Sothern

Ann Sothern, winner of five Emmys, a Golden Globe award and an Academy Award nomination, has been visiting the Valley since 1949. She settled here in 1984. One of Ann's favorites was her role in *Letter to Three Wives*. We thought she was unforgettable in the critically-acclaimed *Whales of August*.

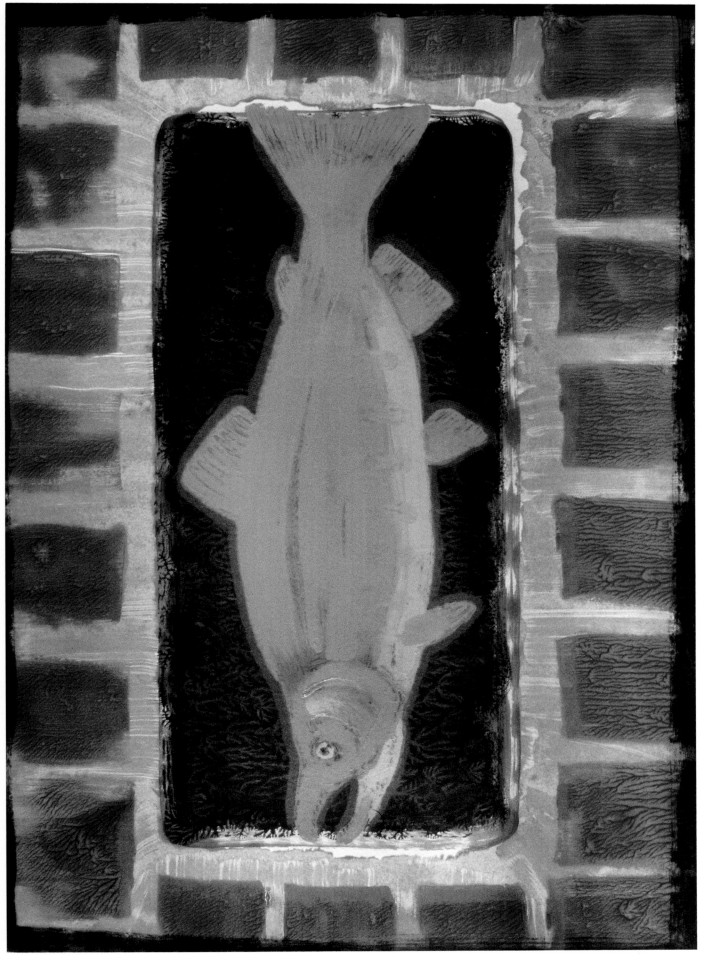

Sockeye Red Alert

Soupçon

My favorite dressing dates back to my days in Aspen, Colorado, at the Copper Kettle, where I began cooking in the 1960s.

CREAMY MUSTARD SALAD DRESSING

Blend ingredients one by one in the order given in food processor or blender:

2 hard boiled eggs
1 1/2 tsp. salt
1 1/2 tsp. sugar
1 tsp. coarse ground pepper
1 tbsp. chopped parsley
1 tbsp. Dijon mustard
1 large clove garlic
1/2 cup olive oil
5 tbsp. heavy cream
1/4 cup wine vinegar

Enjoy fine American and European Cuisine in a Country Setting
Serving an ever changing dinner Menu

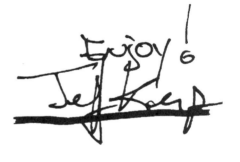

Enjoy!
Jeff Keys

Soupçon

Jeff and Sheila Keys created a feeling of provincial France in downtown Ketchum when they lovingly conceived Soupcon in 1985. In addition to creating culinary masterpieces like Delights of the Naked Stranger, Jeff raises champion appaloosa horses. In 1993, his racing appaloosa was named "World Champion Three-Year-Old Filly."

PECAN WILD RICE

1 cup (1/2 lb.) raw wild rice
5 1/2 cups defatted chicken stock or water

Combine:
1 cup shelled pecan halves
1 cup yellow raisins
grated rind of 1 large orange
1/4 cup chopped fresh parsley
4 scallions, thinly sliced
1/4 cup olive oil
1/3 cup fresh orange juice
1 1/2 tsp. salt
freshly ground black pepper, to taste

1. Put rice in a strainer and run under cold water; rinse thoroughly.

2. Place rice in a medium size heavy saucepan. Add stock or water and bring to a rapid boil. Adjust heat to a gentle simmer and cook uncovered for 45 minutes. After 30 minutes, check for doneness; rice should not be too soft. Drain and transfer rice to a bowl.

3. Add combined ingredients to rice and toss gently. Adjust seasonings to taste. Let mixture stand for 2 hours to allow flavors to develop. Serve at room temperature. Serves 6.

Peggy Grassman

Idaho Special Olympics

In 1993, 800 volunteers coordinated the annual Idaho Special Olympic Winter Games
held in Sun Valley. More than 200 special athletes competed in cross country and downhill events.
Students from north and south county schools joined the athletes as coaches and spirit supporters.
The Winter Games are held in Sun Valley every other year.

Post Office Box 247
Ketchum, Idaho 83340

DISHWASHER FISH

The number this recipe serves depends on the size of the fish or, if small, their number.

1. Whatever the fish, have it cleaned but whole. A salmon done this way is marvelous. Slit the fish along the belly from head to tail.

2. Into the cavity place slices of lemon, chopped parsley, some white wine, salt and pepper to taste, and a sparing amount of such spices and/or herbs as you wish.

3. On a flat surface, roll out enough heavy duty aluminum foil to cover the fish completely when folded over. Wrap the fish in this carefully, crimping all the edges.

4. With another piece of foil, repeat the process so that there is no chance of water leaking into the pouches you have made.

5. Put the fish in your dishwasher, turn on the machine and let it run its full cycle including drying. When ready, remove the fish(es) from the wrappings and serve it hot or refrigerate it and serve it cold. It will be perfectly poached.

Note: This works just as well if the dishwasher is empty or if it contains dishes to be done. Soap or not, makes no difference, provided you have wrapped it correctly.

Clara S. Spiegel

Clara Spiegel

Bald Mountain is now famous for its carpet-like groomed runs, but Clara Spiegel, a resident since the 30s, remembers the rugged, unpacked conditions of the early days. Clara and her husband, a descendant of the Spiegel Catalogue family, joined Ernest Hemingway on one of his African safaris and on fishing outings to Silver Creek. Next time you check out a book in Ketchum, thank Clara, an early founder of Ketchum's Community Library.

CLAM BISQUE SOUP

Makes 12 servings

1 large onion, chopped (1 cup)
6 tbsp. butter
6 tbsp. flour
3 cans (8 oz. ea.) minced clams
2 bottles (8 oz. ea.) clam juice
3 cups light cream
3 tbsp. tomato paste
3 tbsp. lemon juice

1. Saute onion in butter in a large sauce pan until onions are soft. Stir in flour and cook, stirring constantly, just until bubbly.

2. Add clams with liquid, and clam juice. Continue cooking and stirring until sauce thickens. Boil one minute. Cover and simmer 15 minutes.

3. Blend in cream, tomato paste and lemon juice. Heat slowly just until hot.

DAVID R. STOECKLEIN — BOX 856, KETCHUM, IDAHO 83340 — 208-726-5191

David Stoecklein

One of the world's top commercial and stock photographers, David Stoecklein has captured images for Timberland, Coca Cola, Reebok, Wrangler, *Outside Magazine* and almost every ski periodical published. But it is a "soft spot" for cowboy life that has led Dave to publish *The Idaho Cowboy* and *Cowboy Gear,* books honoring the hard work, the sweat, the fatigue and fun way of life many assume has disappeared from the American landscape. Dave's passion for photography and the the wild West takes him "dangerously close to the edge of the light range."

ROSEANNE

This cookie recipe dates from my childhood. On Saturday mornings my brothers and sisters and I would bake. Only half the cookies would make it to the oven. As you will find out, the dough is irresistable. To this day, both the cookies and the dough are family favorites.

Oatmeal Chocolate Chip Cookies

Ingredients:

        3 cups of unbleached white flour
        2 tsp. baking soda
        2 tsp. salt

        1 1/2 cups sugar
        1 1/2 cups brown sugar, packed
        1 cup shortening
        1 cup butter or margerine
        4 eggs, beaten

        4 cups oatmeal
        2 cups (12 oz.) chocolate chips
        1 cup nuts

        2 tsp. vanilla
        1 tsp. water

Directions: Preheat oven to 375 degrees. Cream shortening, butter and sugars well. Beat in eggs, vanilla and water. Sift dry ingredients and add. Next add oatmeal, chocolate chips and nuts. Drop onto ungreased cookie sheets. Bake for 10-12 minutes until golden brown.

Barbara Stoll

Barbara Stoll

4024 Radford Avenue, Bldg. 3 • Studio City, CA 91604 • (818) 760-5135 • FAX (818) 760-5882

Barbara Stoll

Barbara Stoll is co-producer of *ROSEANNE*, a comedy that tackles many tough social and family issues and remains consistently among America's top-rated television shows. During the hard 1993 winter, an avalanche stranded Barbara and her two young children at their cabin for three days. Even after that ordeal, Barbara says, "The Wood River Valley is special ... its beauty revives our souls when life in Los Angeles becomes overwhelming."

ASSOCIATES IN MEDICINE
Sun Valley · Ketchum · Hailey

Sun Valley Office
Sun Valley, (208) 622-4526

Ketchum Office
Ketchum, (208) 726-9361

Hailey Office
Hailey, (208) 788-2412

Sun Valley Sports Medicine
Ketchum, (208) 726-5027

Business Office
(208) 726-9473

Ralph P. Campanale II, M.D.
*General, Vascular
and Thoracic Surgery*

George D. Couris, M.D.
*General, Vascular
and Thoracic Surgery*

Joseph L. Jensen III, M.D.
*Family Practice
and Preventive Medicine*

Stephen R. Luber, M.D.
Pediatrics. Allergy

Royal A. McClure, M.D.
Internal Medicine

P. Scott McLean, Jr., M.D.
Internal Medicine

John A.T. Ross, M.D.
Ear, Nose and Throat

Bryan A. Stone, M.D.
*Family Practice
including Obstetrics*

Eric H. Widell, Jr., M.D.
*Injuries and Disorders
of the Spine*

William L. Brydon, M.D.
Allergy and Asthma

Stephen T. Bushi, M.D.
*Child, Adolescent
and Adult Psychiatry*

Dan S. Fairman, M.D.
Internal Medicine

Gregory L. Flint, M.D.
Dermatology

Timothy Floyd, M.D.
Orthopaedic Surgery

Stephen A. Wasilewski, M.D.
*Orthopaedic Surgery
Arthroscopy and Sports Medicine*

Alison Shearer-Depp, M.D.
Obstetrics and Gynecology

P. O. Box 66
Sun Valley, ID 83353

SMOKEY BEEF BRISKET

ONE WHOLE BEEF BRISKET

PLACE IN A HEAVY 9 x 13 PAN THAT IS A TIGHT FIT

SEAR IN OVEN AT 500° FOR 1/2 HOUR, TURNING ONCE

REMOVE THE MEAT FROM THE PAN AND PUT 1/2 OF THE FOLLOWING IN THE PAN:

- 6 TO 8 ONIONS, SLICED
- 2 TBLSP MUSTARD SEED
- 1 TBLSP CELERY SEED
- 1/2 tsp GROUND PEPPER
- 1 tsp SALT
- 2 CUPS SMOKE-FLAVORED BARBEUE SAUCE

REPLACE THE MEAT IN THE PAN

TOP WITH THE SECOND 1/2 OF THE ONION/SEED/SAUCE MIXTURE

COVER TIGHTLY WITH FOIL

BAKE AT 275° FOR 4 OR 4 1/2 HOURS.

FOR THE NEXT EDITION OF THIS COOKBOOK, PREPARE YOUR PALATES FOR A DELICIOUS RECIPE FOR ROASTED AFRICAN TERMITES.

Bryan Stone, M.D.

Dr. Bryan Stone

For several years in a row, Bryan Stone has been chosen the "Valley's Best Doctor" by his patients and friends. On the national scene, Bryan is the recipient of the "Leadership Award" by a national medical association. Bryan and wife Ann hope to serve soon on an overseas medical mission. "Mangwana Chiremba" — see you later good doctor and friend.

Anchorage, Alaska 415 'F' Street 99501 907/272-1489 FAX 907/272-5395

Seattle, Washington 2030 First Avenue 98121 206/443-1108 FAX 206/443-6580

Sun Valley, Idaho P.O. Box 2237, Ketchum 83340 208/726-4826

I confess, up-front, that I have no recipes to share with you for this cookbook. When I'm painting, wine and potato chips usually tide me over until the urge to do something about dinner passes. However, I eat very well – not because I break down and cook, but because my partner Chuck cooks for both of us. Below is the delicious and colorful dinner that was served to me recently on my 49th birthday.

Shrimp Linguini

20 large fresh shrimp
1/4 lb. butter
1/2 pint heavy cream

4 large cloves of garlic
white wine
1 lb. fresh linguini
1 lemon

Butterfly and devein shrimp and set aside.

Melt butter in large skillet.

Mash garlic between flat of heavy knife and cutting board and add to melted butter.

Saute garlic, stirring constantly on medium-high heat. Remove pan from heat when garlic pieces are browned, then remove and discard the garlic from the butter (be careful not to burn the butter!).

On medium-high heat add shrimp to garlic butter in pan. Quickly saute until edges of shrimp just turn pink (turn shrimp to cook both sides), approximately 30 to 60 seconds on each side.

Immediately remove shrimp from garlic butter and set aside.

Add cream and about 1/2 cup wine to garlic butter.

Saute on medium-high heat, stirring constantly to thicken.

Add salt or garlic salt to taste.

When mixture is thick enough to stick to the linguini, add shrimp back into the mixture and quickly re-heat, stirring constantly (don't overcook them!).

When shrimp are hot, approximately 2 minutes, stir in juice of one lemon and remove from heat, so as not to cook the lemon juice.

Serve immediately over linguini.

Chuck served this with fresh spinach, celery, tomato and egg salad (with Bernstein's Restaurant Recipe Italian Dressing) and Atkinson's Italian bread with garlic and basil (buttered and heated in a 400 oven until hot and crispy).

Nancy Stonington

Nancy Stonington

Since 1971, Nancy Stonington's watercolor art has been displayed in more than 80 one-woman shows from Switzerland to Maui, and from Russia to Alaska. Her works are owned by over 60 corporations, including Alaskan Airlines, AT&T, Rainier Bank and McDonald's. Nancy has a home, studio and gallery in Ketchum.

BANANAS MACHO

Category: dessert   **Servings: six**   **Calories: don't ask**

- 6 - 8 slightly ripe bananas
- 1 qt. french vanilla ice cream
- 1 bar dark chocolate, grated
- 4 tbsp. honey
- 2 cups canola oil
- 2 cups finely sifted flour
- 3 egg whites
- nutmeg, cinnamon

- vanilla extract
- Kahlua or Bailey's Irish Cream
- at least one six pack of Sun Valley White Cloud or Holiday Ale (6 oz. for recipe, the rest for the cook)
- Optional: 1/4 cup brandy

THE SUN VALLEY BREWING CO.

AWARD WINNING BEERS

To make Gordo's not-yet-famous beer batter:

Combine in a deep bowl beer, egg whites, flour, 5 dashes vanilla extract, and one tsp. nutmeg. Mix thoroughly.

Peel bananas and dip them whole, one at a time, into batter mix, coating completely. Put oil in a wok or deep pot. Heat to high. Gently launch bananas into hot oil and fry until golden brown. Have a beer.

Put entire banana batch onto a serving plate, top with grated chocolate, ice cream, honey, ground cinnamon, and your choice of Kahlua or Bailey's.

OR

If you are feeling particularly adventurous, try:

BANANAS ULTRA MACHO

Open another Sun Valley beer. In a small saucepan, heat 1/4 cup brandy until alcohol fumes rise and liquor is hot to the touch. Pour over top of Bananas Macho, quickly check homeowner's policy, and light (the bananas, not the policy). Serve flaming. Good luck.

Gordon M. Gammell
Brewmaster

202 North Main Street · P.O. Box 389 · Hailey, Idaho 83333-389
Phone: (208) 788-5777 · Fax: (208) 788-6319

The Sun Valley Brewing Company

How does a local brew-pub gain national recognition? By winning two gold, three silver and a bronze medal at the national Great American Beer Festival held annually in Denver, Colorado. The Sun Valley Brewing Company, founded in 1986 and located in Hailey, brews up unique blends with indigenous names like White Cloud Ale, Sawtooth Gold Lager and Sun Valley Blonde.

FRANGIPAN CAKE WITH APPLES
(Makes 2)

For the Crust:
1) Cream together til smooth:
8 oz. (1 cup) sugar
12 oz. (3 sticks) butter
pinch of salt

2) Add: (The mixture may separate at this point; it's okay.)
1 egg
1/4 cup milk

3) Add & Mix Smooth:
1 lb. 4 oz. (about 5 cups) flour

Divide dough in 1/2, wrap in plastic, and let rest in cool place 1 hour.

For the Filling:
1) Mix:
2 lb. almond paste
1 lb. butter
3 oz. (1/2 cup) sugar

2) Add & Mix Smooth:
8 eggs

3) Add & Mix Smooth:
3 oz. flour (1/3 cup)

4) Have on hand:
Apricot puree or jam
3 - 4 apples

Put the Cakes Together

Preheat oven to 355°. Lightly spray 2 deep 10" cake pans with vegetable oil.
Roll dough out to 1/8" thick and line both pans completely, piecing the dough together where necessary.
Spread a thin layer of apricot puree or jam on the bottom of the dough-lined pans.
Fill to almost the top with the almond paste mixture.
Spread a thin layer of apricot puree or jam on the top of the almond mixture.
Pare, core, and slice 3 or 4 apples evenly. Make a decorative pattern on the top of the cakes with these.
Sprinkle with a little granulated sugar and bake for about 1 to 1-1/2 hours. (If the apples start to brown too much, cover with foil.)
Cool completely before inverting out of pan.

Compliments of the Chefs

America's First and Finest All Seasons Resort.
Sun Valley Company / Sun Valley, Idaho 83353-0010 / Telephone: 208-622-4111

Sun Valley Company

Early celebrities loved being photographed in Sun Valley and some of those photos hang on the walls of the Lodge, providing a nostalgic walking history of Hollywood. Immortals like Claudette Colbert, Spencer Tracy, Clark Gable, John Wayne, Marilyn Monroe and Ann Sothern came to cavort. Today, stars love coming here to play and to escape the paparazzi. With its world-class ski hill, golf course and year-round activities, Sun Valley is itself a star.

BLACK BEAN TACOS

Ingredients:

2 cups black beans
1 chopped yellow onion
1 strip *Kombu seaweed
2 cloves minced garlic
cayenne to taste
1/2 tsp. cumin
2-3 squirts of *Braggs (liquid amino)

Directions:

Soak beans overnight. Rinse them in a colander and leave to sprout, wetting occasionally. When sprouted, cook in 4 cups water and 1 tsp. sea salt for 1 1/2 hours. Add the remaining ingredients. Cook with the lid off, until the liquid is gone.

Serve in taco shells with a choice of tomato, shredded lettuce, grated cheeses, cilantro, yogurt, sour cream, diced green peppers, etc.

*Kombu seaweed and Braggs can be purchased at health food stores.

P.O. Box 1385
Sun Valley, Idaho 83353
(208) 622-3066

Sun Valley Repertory Company

Kevin McCauley and Ando Hixon filled a cultural void when they founded the Sun Valley Repertory Company in 1992. The beautiful NexStage theatre, a renovated car showroom and garage, has become the artistic soul of the county, hosting comedies, classic and western plays. Renowned actors such as Cliff Robertson and Carol Burnett have performed there.

SUN VALLEY SKI EDUCATION FOUNDATION

Post Office Box 203   Sun Valley, Idaho 83353   (208) 726-4129

SUN VALLEY SKI TEAM LASAGNA

When you're frazzled and need a "quick" dish to feed the entire
neighborhood - - - This is it! The best part is that it's good
when reheated.

10 pcs.	lasagna pasta
48 oz.	jar Prego pasta sauce
15 oz.	ricotta low fat cheese
10 oz.	pkg chopped spinach (thawed & drained)
1 lb.	fresh grated mozzarella cheese
1/2 cup	grated parmesan cheese
2	eggs beaten
	chopped fresh parsley

Cook the noodles (add a bit of oil for non-stick pasta).
Combine: ricotta cheese, spinach, 1/2 cup mozzarella cheese,
          parmesan cheese and eggs. Mix well.

In a 15" x 9" pan layer:

    2 cups sauce
    1/2 of the noodles
    all the cheese/spinach mixture
    mozzarella cheese

add:
    remaining noodles and remaining sauce

Cover with foil. Bake at 350° for 45 minutes. Uncover and add
the remaining mozzarella· and top with parsley. Bake 15
additional minutes. Let stand for 10 minutes. Too easy, huh?

Sun Valley Ski Education Foundation

The Sun Valley Ski Education Foundation has been producing world-class ski racers
like Christin Cooper and Pete Patterson since 1969. Lane Monroe, its director, is a former
U.S. Ski Team coach and United States Ski Coaches' Association master coach.

SUSIE Q RANCH
P. O. BOX 707
PICABO, IDAHO 83348
(208) 788-2590 • (208) 788-3171

CORIANDER CHICKEN SALAD
(Maria Devendorf)

Place a 3 1/2 lb. fryer in a bowl with 4 tbsp. soy sauce. Marinate for at least 2 hours or overnight, turning frequently. Place the fryer, breast down, on a rack and roast in a 425 oven until crisp and brown (about 45 minutes). Strip meat and skin from carcass and cut into 1/4" slivers; chill covered for as long as overnight.

Dressing: Blend 1 tbsp. each of dry mustard and water. Stir in 1/4 cup each of sesame oil (dark) and salad oil, 2 tbsp. lemon juice (fresh), 4 tsp. each of sugar and soy sauce, and 1 tsp. five spice (or 1/2 tsp. cinnamon). Dressing can stand at room temperature, covered, as long as overnight.

Shortly before serving, arrange 5 to 6 cups shredded iceberg lettuce in a 1/2 inch thick bed on a large platter. Combine chicken, 1/4 cup each chopped fresh coriander, sliced green onions, toasted sesame seeds and dressing. Mix with 2 forks until blended. Mound chicken salad in center of lettuce.

PATRICIA G. MILLINGTON

REGISTERED SIMMENTAL

Susie Q Ranch

When Patricia Millington isn't punchin' cattle at the Susie Q Ranch, she is probably growing organic vegetables at the Selway Lodge, an 1898 homestead in the middle of the nation's largest wilderness. The Susie Q arena, nestled in the sagebrush hills east of Picabo, is the site of many local fund-raising benefits and dances attracting such artists as Ian Tyson.

KEVIN SWIGERT

WARBONNET UNLIMITED
STAR ROUTE/FISHER CREEK • KETCHUM, ID 83340 • (208) 774-3369

Alice's Sourdough Hotcakes

First build your sourdough –

Boil half a dozen peeled and cubed potatoes till soft, pour off the liquid and save. Do something interesting with the potatoes like mashed or salad, they,re not part of this recipe.

Mix the cooled potatoe water with unbleached white flour till you have a fairly runny mixture. Let this sit at room temperature for three to five days. Check from time to time to see how it looks. When the mixure begins to bubble and takes on a bold aroma you have fermentation and real sourdough.

You can keep your sourdough going by simply stirring in more flour and letting it "work" or you can place it in the refrigerator to slow it down or the freezer to stop it altogether.

To make hotcakes, place about 2 cups of starter in a bowl. Be sure and replentish your starter by adding more flour and water. Next add soda, shortening, sugar salt and an egg. You will decide how much of each ingredient to add after some experience but a good place to start is 1 teaspoon of soda, 1 tablespoon of vegetable oil, 2 tablespoons of sugar, and a dash and a half of salt. After mixing everything together the batter should be quite runny, if it is to stiff add a little milk.

Heat your griddle to the point where it is just starting to smoke alittle. Pour the batter out to make 5 to 6 inch cakes. Turn them just once when they show good sized bubbles.

Serve the hotcakes with a couple of fried eggs and your own chokecheery syrup.

Kevin Swigert

Kevin Swigert

A fifth-generation Idahoan, stuntman and former U.S. Ski Team member Kevin Swigert must have inherited some tough pioneer genes. He has four times dominated the "Survival of the Fittest," a nationally televised backcountry contest — involving trail running, lake swimming and rappeling — that makes triathlons look like jump rope. One of Kevin's personal-best achievements includes reaching 27,000-feet altitude on the West Ridge of Mount Everest.

Deutsch Brown Trout

Buy 4 trouts, completely gutted. Take some ground parsley and onions and saute them in a good piece of butter. **Add** salt and pepper and fill the trouts with this mixture.

Heat some oil in a frying pan and fry the trouts in the hot oil. **Roast** them on both sides. **Serve** the fish with boiled potatoes, herb butter and a good piece of lemon.

Enjoy your meal.

Claus Cnyrim

Claus Cnyrim
Burgermeister

Tegernsee, Germany

Ketchum's sister city, Tegernsee, sits on the shores of an alpine lake in southern Germany. A ski area is perched in the mountains above. Like Ketchum, its people are friendly and outgoing and sunny days are typical. The sister city designation was established more than 10 years ago as a means for cultural and historical exchange. Burgermeister Claus Cnyrim extends a special invitation to Wood River residents to visit his city.

Caesar's Pasta Salad

Caesar's Salad

12 ounces vermicelli
1 garlic clove, lightly crushed
1 bunch romaine lettuce, sliced crosswise
1/2 cup (or more) fresh grated parmesan cheese
1 cup (or more) herb flavored croutons

Dressing

1/2 cup olive oil
1/4 cup lemon juice
1 raw egg yolk
1/2 tin anchovy fillets, lightly mashed
(reserve other half)
1 teaspoon salt
1/2 teaspoon freshly ground pepper
1/4 teaspoon sugar
1-2 cloves crushed garlic

☆ *Rub a deep serving bowl with one clove of crushed garlic.*

☆ *Cook the vermicelli until al dente, drain, rinse well with cold water and drain thoroughly. Add to the bowl .*

☆ *Blend dressing ingredients in a small bowl.*

☆ *Add dressing, lettuce and 1/4 cup cheese (or more) and toss.*

☆ *Top with croutons, reserved anchovies and remaining cheese and toss lightly.*

We take this dish to a lot of potlucks, and it's always a favorite. Keep the dressing, cheese and croutons on the side and toss it when you're ready to serve. Leave in the anchovies, and don't worry about the kids - they'll eat it anyway!

Cindy and Art Thiede
Art and Cindy Thiede were attracted in 1980 to the Wood River Valley
by the "diversity and abundance of unique log homes." Since settling here,
they have authored two photographic design books titled *American Log Homes*
and *The Log Home Book, Design Past and Present.*

One of my teammates gave me this recipe for "Angry Red Planet" several years ago. Since then, I've fed it to every member of my family, including my (at the time) six month old daughter and many good friends. It's a hearty, tasty and memorable meal.

Angry Red Planet

4 medium beets, peeled and cut into small dice-sized cubes
6 white potatoes, cut same as beets
4 large carrots, sliced into chunks
1 large white or yellow onion
Optional seasonings: fresh, chopped basil or oregano;
tamari or soy sauce
1/3 cup Spanish peanuts, roasted slowly in a small pan. When done, add tamari or soy sauce to coat and turn off the heat.
1/2 cup grated cheddar cheese
2 cups brown rice simmered,
covered, for 45 minutes in 4 cups water

Saute beets in safflower oil on high heat for approximately 10 minutes (add a bit of water if needed to prevent sticking). Add potatoes, onions and carrots and saute for 5 - 10 more minutes. Then cover vegetables with hot water, cover and simmer on high heat until vegetables are soft and almost creamy but still retain their shapes (about one hour, this is a good time to cook your rice). When done the "Planet" will be a bit saucy. Add a pinch of cayenne and serve over brown rice, topped with cheese and peanuts. Serves 6 athletic eaters.

Enjoy!

Katrin Tobin
Santa Cruz, CA

Katrin Tobin

Katrin Tobin grew up in the Warm Springs Canyon. As a child, she spent many Sundays at her "Dad's church" on Baldy. Some of her many prodigious bike-racing accomplishments include winning the 1988 Ore-Ida Women's Challenge, a stage of the 1989 Tour de France Feminin and the 1986 National Road Cycling Championship.

■ ■

GRANDMA SCHERBAN'S CZECHOSLOVAKIAN CABBAGE ROLLS

Saute the following ingredients together:

2 lbs. lean ground beef	2 teaspoons coriander
1/3 lb. ground pork	garlic salt to taste
4 cloves garlic, chopped	fresh ground pepper
1 onion or shallots, chopped	1/2 teaspoon cayenne pepper

Prepare long grain white rice to make 12 servings; mix rice and meat combination.

Cabbage leaves: Cut out the hearts from two heads of cabbage and put heads into pot of boiling water. Boil heads until softened, and when you can, peel the leaves off with tongs one by one, and remove from pot.

Fill each cabbage leaf with about 2 tbsp. of meat and rice mixture and roll up tight like an egg roll or burrito.

You also need 2 large jars of sauerkraut, 4 16-oz. cans of tomato sauce, and 2 lbs. sausage of your choice, chopped into one-inch lengths.

Layer in large pot, as follows: tomato sauce, cabbage rolls, sauerkraut, and sausage, until everything is used.

Optional: smoked ham can be placed in the middle of the pot.

Bake all day at 275. Must be cooked slowly and at low heat, or cabbage will get hard. Cover if top is getting too brown.

This is a great meal for those snowy days when you need to feed a crowd. This meal needs nothing more than a green salad and your favorite red wine. Thanks for sharing your Grandma's recipe, Sandee!

Two Dog Construction

137   Who the heck is Two Dog and why does he think he's a celebrity?

JOHNNY UNSER

LIGHTNING FAST CHICKEN ENCHILADAS -----

COMBINE ---

2	BEATEN EGGS
1c	MINCED COOKED CHICKEN
1c	COOKED DRAINED SPINACH
1/4c	HEAVY CREAM
1	CLOVE GARLIC MINCED
2TBLS	HOT SALSA
1c	JACK CHEESE
1/3c	FRESH GRATED PARMESAN CHEESE
1	4oz. CAN ORTEGA DICED GREEN CHILIS
1	7oz. CAN MILD GREEN CHILI SALSA

FILL --

FILL EACH FLOUR TORTILLA WITH 2TBLS OF MIXTURE, ROLL AND PLACE IN
GLASS BAKING DISH.

TO GARNISH THE TOP USE A SLICED TOMATO AND 3/4c CHEDDAR CHEESE.
OPTIONAL ADD A RED SALSA.

BAKE AT 350 FOR 40 MINUTES

POST OFFICE BOX 2817   SUN VALLEY, ID 83353   TELEPHONE (208) 726-1025

Johnny Unser

Driving faster than lightning Indy race cars and loving "real hot Mexican food" just seem to go together.
Although Johnny may slow down the pace on Highway 75, he still likes the bite of jalapeño.
Johnny is proud to be part of the Unser family, "the winningest family ever in the history of auto racing."

DIANA VOIT

P.O. Box 3367
Ketchum,
Idaho 83340
Fax 208-726-0957

This recipe is a real tradition in my family. The credit goes to my grandmother Cordil, who originated it more than sixty years ago. She always stuffed the turkey with bread dressing, but one of the highlights of the holiday dinners was this wild rice dressing that was cooked and served in a casserole. Often, there were forty or more of us around the tables. Now, most of her fifteen grandchildren, with families of their own, serve this and remember grandma lovingly.

GRANDMA'S WILD RICE DRESSING

1 cup wild rice
4 cups water
1 tsp. salt

Put rice in colander and rinse thoroughly. Bring water to a boil and add salt. Slowly add wild rice and cook until water is absorbed, approximately 40 minutes.

1 lb. seasoned sausage
1 cup onion, chopped
1 cup celery, chopped
1 8-oz. can water chestnuts, chopped
1 4 oz. can sliced button mushrooms (fresh may be used, also)
3/4 cup pecans, chopped
2 tsp. sage

Salt and pepper to taste.
Crumble sausage in 12-inch skillet and cook thoroughly. Add onion and celery to sausage and cook until translucent. Add water chestnuts, mushrooms, pecans, and cooked rice. Mix thoroughly. Add sage and season with salt and pepper to taste.

Serves six.

Diana and Richard Voit

An invitation to dinner at Richard and Diana Voit's north county home is a ticket to a heavenly meal and wonderful camaraderie. Richard is the grandson of William J. Voit, founder of Voit Sporting Goods Company. Voit's first product, introduced just after World War II, was a gigantic beachball.

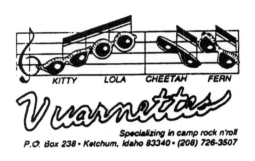

STAND ON YOUR MANICOTTI

To serve 8:
1/2 lb. manicotti (16 shells), boiled and drained
freshly grated Parmesan cheese

Ricotta and mozzarella cheese filling:
2 lb. ricotta or sieved cottage cheese
1/2 lb. mozzarella cheese, diced
2 tbsp. chopped fresh parsley
3/4 tsp. basil
1/2 tsp. salt

Sausage and beef sauce:
*1 lb. Italian sausages, each poked in several places
1 lb. lean ground beef
1 medium-sized onion, finely chopped
4 cups pureed tomato
6 oz. canned tomato paste
1-1/4 cups water
1 tsp. basil
salt
1 tsp. sugar
1/2 tsp. pepper

In a covered Dutch oven over medium heat, cook the sausages in 1/4 cup of the water for five minutes. Uncover; brown the sausages well and drain them on paper towels. Discard the sausage fat, then brown the ground beef with the onion. Stir in the pureed tomato, tomato paste, basil, salt to taste, the sugar, pepper and the remaining water. Cover and simmer for 45 minutes. Cut the sausages into bite-sized pieces and add them to the mixture. Cook for 15 minutes, stirring occasionally.

Meanwhile, preheat the oven to 375. In a large bowl, combine the ricotta or cottage cheese, mozzarella, parsley, basil and salt. Stuff this filling into the cooked manicotti shells.

Spoon half of the meat sauce into one 13x9 inch or two 9 inch square baking dishes. Arrange half of the stuffed shells in one layer on top of the sauce. Spoon most of the remaining sauce, reserving about 3/4 cup, over the shells; top with the remaining shells in one layer. Spoon the reserved meat sauce over the top. Sprinkle the manicotti with grated Parmesan cheese. Bake for 30 minutes in the preheated oven.

*Oddly enough, not one of us has made it past this step.
Please let us know how it turns out!

The Vuarnettes

While performing a multitude of daily domestic duties, it dawned on the Vuarnettes that things could be different. The lives of each Vuarnette, "Cheetah Velveetah," "Lola Motorola," "Kitty Litter" and "Fern Find-a-Buck," changed dramatically and forever when they stopped being maids, put on their shades and started singing raucous lyrics and performing bawdy comedy. Here, with a tip of their hats to Tammy Whynot is "Stand on Your Manicotti."

Sourdough Scone Recipe

Yields 100 Scones

Ingredients:

1 package dry yeast	½ cup dry skim milk powder
¼ cup warm water	2-4 tablespoons vegetable oil
2 tablespoons sugar	1½ cups thick sourdough starter
2 teaspoons salt	1½ cups water
	4 cups flour

Soften yeast in ¼ cup warm water. Combine sugar, salt, milk powder and oil with the 1½ cup of water in a large mixing bowl. Add yeast mixture and sourdough starter to water mixture, blend gently. Gradually add flour and knead until smooth. (More flour may be necessary.) Place in a greased bowl and let rise to double in size. (1½ to 2 hours.)

Turn out onto lightly floured board and divide into 2-3 oz. pieces. Roll out flat. Let rest and deep fat fry at 375° until golden brown.

Honey Butter

⅓ honey - ⅓ butter - ⅓ margarine

Melt above ingredients while mixing over low heat. Remove from stove and stir while cooling. Pour into cups or molds and refrigerate.

Michael Simpson

P.O. Box 5507, Ketchum, Idaho 83340 208-726-2609

Warm Springs Ranch Restaurant

Originally named Warm Springs Ranch Inn, the former potato farm was purchased by Owen Simpson in the late 40s and was converted to a horse and cattle ranch. Private fish ponds were established which made it a picturesque site for a restaurant, which was built in 1953. Patrons could catch their dinner from the well-stocked trout ponds. The present day tennis club was the site of the rodeo grounds used by the locals in the 50s. This uniquely scenic property is still owned by the Simpson family.

141

ADAM WEST

```
                 SAWTOOTH
        CAST IRON SKILLET POT ROAST


Suggested for those times when the man of the house
finds himself in the kitchen expected to do something
wonderful or reasonably satisfying and nutritious:



Ingredients-      One large chuck or 7-bone roasting
                  cut of beef, elk, moose or other.
                  Four large onions.
                  A large garlic clove.
                  Herb salts and seasonings.
                  Two celery stalks.
                  One apple.
                  A few dates or raisins.
                  Potatos, at least one per diner.
                  Carrots, at least one per diner.
                  One package frozen green peas.

Season roast well. Braise in olive oil and butter in
black cast iron skillet while adding halved onions and
peeled garlic. Do not burn onions and garlic. Add some
garlic inserted in roast. Sprinkle a bit of dried peppers
here and there. Preheat oven to 400 degrees. When meat is
well braised on stove kill burner and add enough hot water
to submerge some carrot slices and potato chunks (the rest
you will par-boil and add later when meat shrinks a bit to
give you more room in skillet). Add cut up unpeeled apple
to top of roast and in liquid. Slip a few raisins or dates
into cracks in meat. Transfer skillet to oven. This move
should be made carefully and soberly because your skillet
will be quite heavy and hot by this time. Cover with foil.
Cook three or four hours until meat falls apart with fork.
Add water when needed. About an hour before done to taste,
add par-boiled vegetables to cook further in juices. Sea-
son a bit more if you wish. Remove foil for a bit to
further brown contents. Ten minutes before removing, add
green peas (thawed) to center of roast in attractive
pattern. Recover with foil. Turn off oven and serve from
skillet with some sour-dough biscuits which you can dip
in liquid or make gravy, too. Best part: very little to
clean up!
```

Adam West (signature)

Adam West

Look in Sun Valley's *Names and Numbers* telephone book under Batman, and you'll see **West, Adam**.
Look under West, Adam and read: See **Wayne, Bruce (Millionaire)**. Check Wayne, Bruce (Millionaire)
and you'll be directed to **Crime Fighters in the Yellow Pages**. From the Yellow Pages, the trail circles
back to: **Batman**. The 1960s television show is seen by a 1/2 billion people across the world in reruns.
The Caped Crusader, aka Adam West, lives in Ketchum.

WAGON TRAIN BISCUITS AND GRAVY

BISCUITS

        APPROXIMATELY 30-32 CUPS OF FLOUR
        1 CUP OF SUGAR
        4 TABLESPOONS SALT
        14 HEAPING TABLESPOONS BAKING POWDER
        1 1/2 POUNDS MARGARINE
        16 CUPS OF BUTTERMILK

MIX DRY INGREDIENTS. MELT MARGARINE AND ADD TO DRY INGREDIENTS. ADD
BUTTERMILK AND MIX THOROUGHLY. POUR OUT ONTO FLOURED BOARD. ADD
FLOUR AND KNEAD UNTIL DOUGH IS NOT TACKY.(DON'T OVER-MIX!!!) ROLL
OR PAT OUT UNTIL THE DOUGH IS 1 1/4 INCHES THICK. CUT OUT WITH
SMALL SOUP CAN. GREASE PAN. PLACE BISCUITS IN PAN LEAVING SOME ROOM
FOR GROWTH. PREHEAT OVEN @ 375. BAKE FOR 20-30 MINUTES UNTIL GOLDEN
BROWN.

GRAVY

        8 QUARTS MILK
        1 1/2 POUNDS PORK SAUSAGE
        4 TEASPOONS THREE PEPPER(USE BLACK AND RED AS SUBSTITUTE)
        1/4 CUP GARLIC POWDER
        1/4 CUP SEASONED SALT
        2 TABLESPOONS ONION POWDER
        ROUX-MIXTURE OF VEGETABLE OIL AND FLOUR

BROWN PORK SAUSAGE. ADD SPICES. ADD MILK AND BRING TO ALMOST
BOILING. STIR OCCASIONALLY TO KEEP BOTTOM FROM BURNING. ADD ROUX
PROGRESSIVELY AND WHIP VIGOROUSLY TO KEEP MIXTURE SMOOTH. ADD MORE
ROUX TO THICKEN IF NECESSARY.

Jack & Jeanne Greenberg

Western Cafe

Clint Eastwood, Ernest Hemingway and Brooke Shields have all savored country breakfasts
and the homey atmosphere of the Western Cafe. The cafe has been serving biscuits and
143   gravy in the same location on Main Street, Ketchum since 1953.

LUKE WHALEN, D.D.S.
116 W. Bullion P.O. Box 1149
Hailey, Idaho 83333
___
Telephone: (208) 788-4507

SESAME FRIED LEMON PHEASANT

1 1/2 cups milk	2 tsp. grated lemon zest
2 1/2 tbsp. lemon juice	1 tsp. salt
4 pheasant breasts, skinless	1 tsp. ground black pepper
1/4 cup yellow cornmeal	3 tbsp. butter
1/4 cup all purpose flour	3 tbsp. vegetable oil
1/4 cup sesame seeds	thin lemon slices for garnish

1. In a non-reactive dish, combine the milk and lemon juice. Add the pheasant and marinate, covered in the refrigerator for about an hour.

2. In a shallow dish combine the cornmeal, flour, sesame seeds, lemon zest, salt and pepper. Remove the pheasant from the marinade, but do not pat dry. Dredge the pheasant in the cornmeal mixture to coat completely.

3. In a large skillet melt the butter and oil over moderately high heat. Add the pheasant and fry, turning once, until deep golden brown on both sides (six to eight minutes depending on size). Drain on paper towel and transfer to warm platter. Garnish with lemon slices.

Luke Whalen

Luke Whalen, aka "The Wild Gourmet," taught budding gourmands how to cook on local Channel 13 during the 1980s. He is a member of the board of directors for Pheasants Forever, a nationwide conservation group dedicated to providing habitat for wild animals.

THE WOLF EDUCATION & RESEARCH CENTER

The Wolf Education and Research Center was founded in 1990 by Jim Dutcher and Karen McCall as a result of their experience making a documentary on the gray wolf for ABC television. The Center's primary goal is to give people a chance to watch and learn about the Sawtooth Wolf Pack. This first-hand experience will be complimented by a host of educational programs that discuss wolf biology, other endangered species, the ecology of the Northern Rockies, and the necessity of maintaining the region's biodiversity.

Until the Center's facility is completed near Galena Lodge, the 6 members of the Sawtooth Wolf Pack are in a large 20 acre enclosure in the Stanley Basin. Because this part of Idaho is notorious for being the coldest spot in the nation, soup and bread are often the fare served to patrons and occasional guests. This soup is always a good choice. It's tasty and colorful and the red chilis add a bit of bite.

Red Pepper Soup

Serves 4-6

Kristin Poole
Director
Wolf Education and Research Center

8 red peppers
3 carrots, peeled
3 shallots, peeled
1 pear, peeled and quartered
1 Tbs. Olive oil
4 Tbs. Butter
1 clove garlic, peeled
1 quart chicken or vegetable stock
1/2 t. crushed red pepper chilis
Dash of cayenne
Salt and pepper to taste
Sprigs of fresh tarragon to taste

• Thinly slice 6 of the peppers, the carrots, shallots, garlic and pear.
• Heat oil and butter in a large skillet and saute the sliced vegetables and pear over medium low heat until tender.
• Add the stock, red pepper, cayenne, salt and pepper. Bring to a boil and simmer, covered, for 25 to 30 minutes.
• While soup is cooking, roast the remaining red peppers.
• Puree the soup in a food processor or blender, adding one of the roasted peppers. Pour soup back into pan and reheat over a low flame.
• Julienne the remaining pepper and add to the soup. Garnish with tarragon (or a dollop of sour cream) and serve.

Kristin Poole

POST OFFICE BOX 3832 · KETCHUM, IDAHO 83340 · TELEPHONE 208-726-2860 · FAX 208-726-2747

The Wolf Education & Research Center

Jim Dutcher and Karen McCall founded the Wolf Education and Research Center in 1990 after making a documentary on the gray wolf for ABC television. The Center's primary goal is to give people a chance to watch and learn, firsthand, about the Sawtooth wolf pack. Until the Center's facility is completed near Galena Lodge, the wolf pack's six members live in a large 20-acre enclosure in the Stanley Basin.

Congratulations to the Advocates for Survivors of Domestic Violence. Your work is to be commended for all your assistance and support for the women and children in the Wood River Valley suffering from domestic abuse.

kristi yamaguchi

SWEET AND SOUR CHICKEN WINGS

3 lbs. chicken wings

Cut into sections. Sprinkle with garlic salt and let sit for 1 hour.

Sauce:

3/4 cup sugar
1/2 cup vinegar
1 tbsp. soy sauce
3 or 4 tbsp. catsup

Combine the sauce ingredients and cook until the sugar dissolves.

Roll chicken in cornstarch. Beat 2 eggs and dip chicken into egg mixture. Deep fry until light brown.

Dip the fried chicken in the sauce and lay the pieces in a shallow pan.

Bake in 300□ oven for about 45 minutes.

Kristi Yamaguchi

When Kristi Yamaguchi jumps on the ice at the Sun Valley Ice Show all chatter stops. From then on, the crowd is mesmerized by the talent that earned the twenty-some year old a gold medal for her overall skating performance at the 1992 Olympics. Kristi has returned to Sun Valley for five summers, and her shows are always an early sellout.

For 4 people

RISOTTO WITH ARTICHOKES AND PEAS

10 baby artichokes
1 lb. fresh peas (or 10 oz. frozen)
1 glass of white wine
2 cloves garlic
1/2 cup chopped parsley
4 tabsp. olive oil
1/2 onion, chopped
2 cups Arborio rice
6 cups (approx.) chicken stock

Remove outer, dark leaves from artichokes and discard. Trim 1/4"
off top of remaining leaves. Thinly slice artichokes vertically
and saute in olive oil with chopped onion for 4 minutes. Quickly
add the chopped garlic and parsley, stir 1/2 minute (do not burn
garlic), then add the rice. Stir again and add wine and cook until
it evaporates. Finish cooking the risotto by adding 2 cups of
simmering stock to rice, stirring to avoid bottom of pan burning,
until absorbed. Add more stock as necessary until rice is tender
and creamy. Add the peas five minutes before done. Serve with
plenty of grated parmesan cheese.

SPAGHETTI PESTO DE LUXE

For 4 people

Mix in food processor:

1/2 cup pine nuts	1 lb. spaghetti, cooked
1/3 cup walnuts	1/2 cup grated Romano cheese
2 cloves of garlic	1/2 cup grated Parmesan
30 leaves of fresh basil	
3/4 cup good olive oil	
salt and pepper	

Process well and mix with cooked spaghetti, adding 1/2 cup grated
parmesan and 1/2 cup grated romano cheeses. Garnish with pitted,
marinated black olives.

Richard D. Zanuck   Lili Zanuck

202 North Canon Drive, Beverly Hills, California 90210 (310) 274-0261 Fax: (310) 273-9217
200 West 57th Street, New York, New York 10019 (212) 246-2660 Fax: (212) 765-2948

Richard and Lili Zanuck

Richard and Lili of the Zanuck Company take a one-dimensional script and after many
months of sweat, hand us heartfelt classics like *Cocoon, The Sting* and *Driving Miss Daisy* or
nightmare-inducing movies like *Jaws*. Richard first came to Sun Valley when he was three
years old, and he and Lili now live here. Richard says, "Unlike most other resorts,
I find Sun Valley much more relaxed and unassuming."

Will Caldwell

Will Caldwell lives with his family on the back side of Baldy and has shown his art locally and nationally since 1975. The search for painting subjects has led him to five continents and his work has been shown in a dozen western states. His paintings are in collections as diverse as the National Archives of Kenya, George Lucas in Hollywood, or the Coca Cola Corporate Museum in Florida.

Will was raised in Oregon, graduated from Oregon State University, and has studied with some of the American West's most renowned artists. At the time of this printing, his paintings are on exhibit in galleries in Los Angeles, Telluride, Colorado, and in the Kneeland Galleries in Ketchum and Las Vegas. The paintings and sketches reproduced here are a mix of Will's recent themes. The animals reflect his commitment as an outspoken activist for conservation; the nostalgia images recall the America he grew up in.

Bellevue Polo Ponies

INDEX

Continued next page

ORDER FORM

Please send the *Sun Valley Celebrity & Local Heroes Cookbook* to:

Send to Name: _____

Address: _____

City: _____ State: _____

Zip: _____ Telephone: (_____) _____

Price	Quantity	Total
$12.00	_____	$ _____
	Shipping & handling $4.00 per book	$ _____
	Total enclosed	$ _____

Please make checks payable to The Advocates
Please do not send cash. Sorry, no C.O.D.'s

Please charge my: ☐ Visa ☐ MasterCard

Acct#: _____ Expiration Date: _____

Cardholder's Signature: _____

Sent by Name: _____

Address: _____

(Fill out only if different from above "send to" name.)

City: _____ State: _____

Zip: _____ Telephone: (_____) _____

Profits from the sale of this cookbook are used to support community projects of the Advocates for Survivors of Domestic Violence. The Advocates for Survivors of Domestic Violence is a non-profit group committed to the idea that all Wood River families deserve to live in safety and dignity.

The Advocates have helped hundreds of families through their counseling and support group programs, court advocacy and crisis hotline. With a 24-hour crisis hotline, each volunteer advocate is at the front line of domestic violence.

Advocates respond to crises at the hospital, the police station or where ever they are needed to offer women or men the options they need to make healthy decisions in their lives.

Send to: **The Advocates, P.O. Box 3216, Hailey, ID 83333**

(208) 788-4191